Explo*

Sacred Space

A Vast Quest

PISS
GReat
INDICATOR

Kristen Ann

Revised 1/10/12

Cover Art by the author is titled *Sacred Space*. The original is 40" x 30" oil on canvas.

Lithographs of the cover artwork, as well as this book, are available at ExploringSacredSpace.com. Illustrations in the book can also be seen in color on this site.

VastQuestVentures@gmail.com

ISBN 978-0-615-49890-4

Contents

Before We Start   i

Acknowledgements   ii

Dedication   iii

Illustrations   iv

1. When You're Ready the Teacher Will Come   1

2. An Enigmatic Lesson   8

3. Extraordinary Times, Extraordinary Beings   19

4. An Otherworldly Event   24

5. Another Class: Revelations Continue   40

6. Exploring a Multi-Faceted Universe   46

7. The Teaching Unfolds   68

8. Days of Merlin and Arthur: Pivotal Moment in Time   74

9. More Revelations and Instructions to Prepare for the Future   82

10. A Little Spiritual Cosmology   97

11. Other Beings Playing a Part   102

12. Meeting Dan Fry   113

13. Surgeon from Another World?   124

14. Dinner with an Alien?   133

15. A Mysterious Time Loss Incident   137

16. "Coincidental" Meeting and More Verification   144

17. The Power of Meditation   152

18. A Harp Story   158

19. Experiences in Egypt   171

20. Clues to the Egyptian Mysteries   184

21. A Pre-Destined Crystal   192

22. The Maltese Connection   202

23. The Spring Full Moon Festivals   205

24. Halfway to Heaven   209

Resources and Books   216

About the Author   219

Before We Start

The purpose for writing this book is to give a different perspective of our point in history, presenting an alternative view of what is going on now and why. Many fear-based and speculative scenarios have been given for 2012. This information comes from far more accurate and reliable sources than those speculations.

This writing will elaborate on the world situation and what has led to it. It will also give reliable scenarios of the future on planet Earth, what to expect and a little bit about how to prepare. Most significantly it will offer scenarios of future events based on more than speculation.

My goal is to inform and prepare people. Most importantly I would like to share an understanding of our point in time as well as a view of what lies ahead. It is my hope that we, the residents of Earth, broaden our awareness of the *truth* of life at its deepest levels. We live in a multi-faceted and multi-dimensional universe.

Everything in this book is a true account, stated exactly as it happened.

"There are more things in heaven and earth, Horatio, than are dreamt of in your philosophy." Shakespeare, from *Hamlet*.

In Light, Peace and Understanding,

Kristen

Acknowledgements

Three people have been invaluable to me in finalizing this book. I could not have done this without the superb editing and advising help from Robert (Bob) Durant, Diane Dyann and my sister, Lisa.

Hugs to you all! Thank you.

Dedication

    I found this image on my first trip to Egypt in 1997. It was on the walls of many of the ancient temples and palaces. For some reason the image resonated deeply with me.

    Standing in the Cairo Museum one day, I found myself staring again at this glyph. When I asked our Egyptian guide, Emil Shaker, what it meant he said it means "Eternally Living Child of God", and that it was an emblem of royalty.

    This book is dedicated to the Eternally Living part in all of us.

Illustrations

See Images in color at ExploringSacredSpace.com

1a	Werner Glas	2	6m	Mysterious curved disk	59
1b	Rudolf Steiner	7	6n	Flower of Life, Osirian	60
2a	Wheel of Ages	10	6o	Leonardo's notes	61
2b	Seneca Wheel	12	6p	Thirteen circles	62
2c	Avenue of the Sphinxes	13	6q	Wall of vehicles	63
2d	Coptic Temple Fish	14	6r	Assissi Church	66
4a	Alice A. Bailey	29	7a	Graph of the rays	71
4b	Franz Bardon	33	8a	Merlin's cave	78
6a	Akhenaten's Daughters	48	8b	Madonna of the Rocks	80
6b	Egyptian Bust	49	12a	Dan Fry's Tonapah res.	115
6c	Nefertiti	49	12b	Dan and Florence Fry	116
6d	Syrian Gods	50	15a	Mom at White Sands	144
6e	"Boat of Sokar"	51	18a	Antique zither harp	166
6f	Ptah in his bodysuit	52	18b	Horus and I at Edfu	172
6g	Hathor	53	19a	Hand of Osiris	184
6h	Hathor in her vehicle	54	20a	George McMullen	189
6i	Light bulbs at Dendera	55	20b	Artifact necklace	191
6j	Thoth writing on a Tablet	56	21a	Sunrise at Paraiso	199
6k	Ptah and other gods	57	21b	Quartz crystal	203
6l	Thoth with red disk	57	22a	Ari the Maltese	208

1

When You're Ready
the Teacher Will Come

His intense eyes pierced into our souls on that fall afternoon. There were a few frozen moments of silence, and it felt as if time itself stood still. Our eyes were focused on Werner's eyes as we waited for him to continue. That day our world and our entire belief systems would change.

"Could this be **true**?" I was thinking ... yet something at the depth of my soul affirmed it was all completely true and accurate -- and these were revelations of the Truth at its very core. Every amazing concept Werner told us had an unmistakable ring of truth to it.

Werner was master of the dramatic pause. He would present mind-blowing concepts and then we'd all sit there suspended while his intense dark eyes gazed at us in silence. They were eyes that seemed endlessly deep, as if they connected to other dimensions ... eyes filled with a quality of wisdom and understanding that I've never found in anyone else.

1a Werner Glas -- This picture doesn't really show the depth and intensity of Werner's eyes. They were very much like Rudolf Steiner's.

Werner's pauses spoke volumes. Each one would underscore the importance of what he said or what he was about to say.

His classes were incredible. Werner knew the deepest secrets about the very origin of life and the universe. It was information we never could have imagined, and once again he had us on fire with curiosity -- listening intently to each word.

The year was 1974. I had just turned 20 and was starting two years of studies at the most fascinating school of higher learning. It was the Waldorf Teacher Training Institute, which at that time was in Detroit. Werner Glas started the Institute and was our head professor. And he was the most extraordinary person I've ever known.

Werner had a rare gift -- the gift of spiritual sight known as clairvoyance. Every feature of his being portrayed the unique person he was. This was very rare especially in the '70s. He had the striking profile of Alfred Hitchcock and spoke with a deep, rich, resonant voice. It was a striking voice, intensified even more by his British accent and the slow, calculated way he spoke. And there was much more that made this man unique.

Clairvoyance is sharpened perception allowing one to sense things from a distance. It has been called remote viewing or being psychic. In older times it was known as spiritual sight.

Scientists have determined that most of us are using only 5 to 10 percent of our brain's capacity. I believe someone who has sharpened perceptions of clairvoyance is using more of the brain's potentials. Those with very sharpened clairvoyance can even *see* the distant past as well as the future.

In our classes Werner seemed to know if we understood what he said. He had this very dramatic way of looking at us sometimes after he'd make a provocative statement. Often after he made a profound statement he would look at us with his head slightly bent downward, peering enigmatically up at us above the frames of his glasses with those jet black eyes. I came to realize that he could see auras better without looking through his thick lenses and somehow the slight changes in our auras would indicate to him whether or not this information was registering with us.

This man would have been a wonderful actor. He had studied drama in England in fact. Drama was a natural part of who Werner was, and it made our studies all the more fascinating and intense.

I'm writing this because as time goes on this incredible information, seen through the eyes of the clairvoyant truth of what IS, becomes more and more significant -- and needed. Much of it deals with both the past and future of Earth and humanity. It will bring an understanding from a different perspective of what is happening in the world, and why. This is information learned both from classes at the Institute as well as from experiences in my life that followed. This perspective goes beyond the fear-based and speculation about 2012. There are details given here that won't be found anywhere else.

I will start by presenting a few very significant lessons from the Institute.

****

As students there we all sensed the deep truth behind what we were learning. When you're learning from the gift of clairvoyance or spiritual knowing it is truth at its deepest level. It may seem hard to understand but strong clairvoyant ability allows a person to see exactly what *IS* -- past, present and future. There is a profound level of clairvoyance where no speculation is involved. One instantly *knows* and can *see* the truth and what simply *IS* or *will be*.

The Waldorf system of education is based on the clairvoyant genius Rudolf Steiner. He had the most profoundly sharpened clairvoyant ability of anyone I've heard of. He was born in 1861 in Austria and died in 1925, yet he was very much ahead of his time and a very significant soul who did much for the good of humanity.

Steiner was an inventor and made breakthroughs in nearly every field including science, medicine, teaching and even the arts. This included a form of dance called Eurythmy. This form of dance beautifully expresses the movement and gestures of spiritual energy. Rudolf Steiner taught that each

5

sound creates a spiritual gesture or movement. He could see into these other dimensions or planes.

I found it especially interesting to see the gestures formed by a name, as each letter has a specific gesture. This is the gesture we come into a life with -- our name.

1b Rudolf Steiner

Studying life from Steiner's perspective of seeing the spiritual planes was amazing and so richly valuable. It gave an in-depth understanding to the many layers of existence. This expanded view cannot be gained from regular studies. It's been called the "Science of Spirit", and was way ahead of its time. Scientists now recognize the existence of other dimensions or levels to life.

Steiner's philosophy of spiritual science is called Anthroposophy. He used his sharp gifts of clairvoyance to help people and humanity as a whole, broadening our knowledge and understanding of life at its deepest levels. Steiner was invited to lecture at the Waldorf Astoria cigar factory. Workers there asked questions on many topics including education. Steiner shared a depth of knowledge with them in many different areas. They recognized his rare insight and ability to bring out the best in people. Rudolf Steiner was then asked to create a better school system. One that would make the most of children's abilities and learning capacity. This is how the Waldorf system of education began.

It is a system which both takes advantage of and enhances the innate qualities of children. Creativity and art are strongly emphasized, especially in the younger grades. It was found that this strengthens the brain's ability to be more creative in thought processes throughout life. By having an early immersion in art, where the creative and imaginative parts of the brain are enhanced, those children surpass students in other schools with higher scores in later grades.

There are many Waldorf Schools as well as Waldorf-related Institutes and colleges for higher learning around the world, though there will never be another Werner Glas. It was a case of being at the right place and time to have studied with him.

2

An Enigmatic Lesson

"We are living at a time of Noah!" Werner's resounding voice filled the room with this paradoxical statement.

We sat there mesmerized, lost in the depths of Werner's dark hypnotic eyes. A seriousness in his attitude that day revealed the importance of this lesson. His statement sparked our curiosity, as usual, and we sat there in silence wondering what in the world he meant by this. Taking a slow deep breath, Werner continued.

"This is a crucial time in the history of the planet, and you've all chosen to be here at this point in time."

Werner walked to the side of the room and pulled down a screen. He turned on a projector and a large horizontal oval appeared. At the top it was labeled, "The Great Wheel of Ages, 25,920 years".

"This Great Wheel of Ages was drawn up and used by the ancient Hindus and Tibetans," he explained. "It has been verified as accurate by Rudolf Steiner himself as well as by other clairvoyants over the years. This diagram actually depicts two types of wheels superimposed. The ancient Hindus and Tibetans divided their wheel into eight ages they called yugas. Their wheel is on the outer edge. Along the inner edge the wheel is divided into twelve ages with the familiar Greek zodiac names."

"One entire revolution of the wheel is 25,920 years. The Hindus and Tibetans actually use four different yugas or ages, which mirror themselves on each side of the wheel. This makes eight yugas in all. The Kali Yuga on the left edge is the shortest, and there are two Kali Yugas back to back. Each yuga gets progressively longer, with the Satya Yuga on the right side being the longest. Again there are two Satya Yugas back to back."

"We are now at this point on the lower left edge", Werner pointed to the circle indicating our present point in time at the lower left of the wheel. It's important to note that this Wheel of Ages progresses counter-clockwise, and the Ages also seem to progress "backwards" from the way the zodiac months go. So we're moving from the Piscean Age into the Aquarian Age."

The Wheel of Great Ages: 25,920 years. A full cycle of our Solar System thru the constellations. Two wheels superimposed. The original Hindu-Tibetan Yugas outer edge, Greek Zodiac Ages interior.

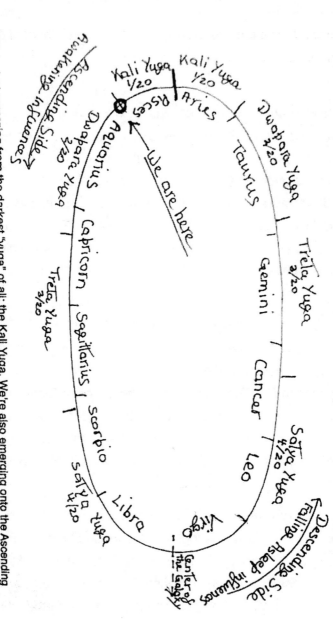

We're just emerging from the darkest "yuga" of all: the Kali Yuga. We're also emerging onto the Ascending and Awakening side of the wheel, as well as emerging into the more enlightened Age of Aquarius.

2a Wheel of Ages.

"From the Hindu and Tibetan standpoint we are now emerging from the influence of the Kali Yuga, which is the darkest and most materialistic Age of the whole wheel. The Dark Ages happened over this period of Kali Yuga, as well as a steady increase in materialism. Most books in our libraries have been written under the influence of the Kali Yuga."

This was 1974. The vast range of "New Age" books had not yet been written. I just remember being struck by the statement -- and I realized how true it was. Most books that filled library bookshelves then, and most books up until the later seventies, were written by people who came from the old ways of thinking and understanding. Werner again pointed to the lower left edge of the wheel.

"We are emerging from the less enlightened Kali Yuga of the Hindus and Tibetans, and we're also feeling the influences of moving into the more enlightened Aquarian Age. In addition to this we are also emerging onto the "Ascending" side of the Wheel. The upper side of the wheel is the "Descending" side. Over this roughly 13,000 year period an underlying current exists of descending into a life of more struggles and less enlightenment or awakening."

"The lower side of the Wheel is the Ascending side. The underlying current felt throughout these 13,000 years is one of ascension and positive growth. Our lives at this point in time will be under this influence of awakening."

I'm breaking from the class here to show you the native American Seneca Wheel of Ages which corresponds with the Hindu/Tibetan one. To the Seneca shamans each age was seen as a new period of evolution or awakening. They drew their wheel in a circle, dividing it into seven Ages they call "Worlds".

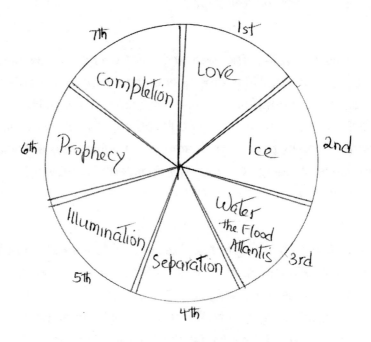

2b Seneca Wheel

According to the Seneca we are just passing from the World of Separation into the World of Illumination, which will begin in 2012 with a thousand years of peace. They believe that there is a short "Time of No TIme" between each world. The duration of the wheel corresponds with the 25,920 years as seen by the ancient Hindu, Tibetans and also by modern scientists. I'll list some interesting beliefs of a few other native American tribes.
Inca talk of the "return of the Luminous One" in 2012.

Lakota have a tradition of "star bundles" which could reflect extra-terrestrial contact. The Lakota have two star maps.

Chief Seattle said "Man has forgotten when he walked among the stars."

Omaha had two sacred pipes. One for those with a "star origin".

The Mayans believed that the process of growth did not change. It was mankind's consciousness that changed as he moved toward perfection. They believed a cycle will be completed on December 21, 2012 when the sun will receive a powerful ray of light from the galaxy's center. They said this will create a cosmic event thrusting mankind into a new Golden Age. We will then be ready to pass through the door left by them, transforming our civilization from fear-based to one with a much higher vibration.

"Ancient people had a better understanding of the Ages and the teacher who came at the start of each Age. Moses ushered in

2c Avenue of Sphinxes. *I took this photo in Luxor in November 1997. It is similar to the one Werner then showed us as he continued this class.*

the Age of Aries. The great temples at Luxor had an avenue lined with Ram's headed sphinxes which went from Karnak to the Luxor temple. The rams-headed sphinxes were a tribute to the Age of Aries, which was when they were constructed. Later Jesus came to usher in the Age of Pisces and the fish became a symbol associated with him in honor of the Piscean Age."

2d *A wall relief from a Coptic Christian temple in Egypt, indicating the Piscean Age*

"This whole progression of 25,920 years continues over and over. It progresses in an upward spiral. With each cycle of the wheel mankind awakens and evolves a little further. There are always periods of digressing or going backward a little in growth, but on the whole, life is an upward spiral of progression."

"The entire duration of 25,920 years is the time it takes for our solar system to make a complete cycle thru the twelve constellations of the zodiac. The zodiac ages actually vary in duration from around 900 years at the shortest to around 2,000 years each, though they may be drawn to look equal here. Some people who have been familiar with this time wheel did not realize that the twelve zodiac ages actually vary in length. As a result there has been some confusion about when certain ages took place and which age we're heading into now. The fact is we're just leaving the more traditional Piscean Age and heading into the more awakened Aquarian Age, which will last roughly 2,000 years."

We all sat there fascinated. The popular *Age of Aquarius* song from the late '60s was making more sense. We now had a new understanding of what this meant. Mind-blowing as this all was, the most intriguing part of the lesson was still to come. Werner pointed again to the bottom left side of the wheel and then continued.

"The point where we are now is about 900 years from the left end. And this is important. It's about 900 years from either end of this Wheel that the full momentum. It is at these points the influence of that side of the wheel -- of either Ascending or Descending -- is felt more fully. In our case the Ascending or Awakening influence is sharply increasing now, and over the next few decades this influence will be felt by society more and more."

15

Once again, the year was 1974, and this statement has certainly become a reality. Individuals and groups have steadily increased in awareness and sensitivity. Thousands of New Age books have been written which have investigated the deeper meanings of life, and topics such as healing and latent human abilities.

Werner stood leaning against the front of his desk. It seemed like he was assessing how best to tell us the next part. After another long breath, his eyes met ours with a sense of gravity and he continued.

"It is also at these points of about 900 years from either end of this Wheel that major events occur."

He looked at us in silence again for a few moments as the room took on a very hushed ambiance. It felt like we were being entrusted with deep secrets of the utmost importance.

"At these points there is a type of catastrophe or Earth cataclysm. It's the natural course of nature for a cataclysm to take place at these times. This has happened roughly every 13,000 years throughout history."

Werner paused, looking at us again. I sensed that he was taking stock of whether or not we understood or had any questions. This time his demeanor was especially focused, revealing the importance of this information.

"Any guesses what happened 13,000 years ago?"

Werner's eyebrows lifted and his expression became more upbeat. There wasn't a sound in the class. We were still trying to digest all this new information and to imagine what major event would have happened 13,000 years ago. He took a step forward and continued.

"What happened roughly 13,000 years ago was the Great Flood." Again there was a pause.

"The Great Flood is an event that really *did* happen. It has been recorded by many different cultures around the globe. Some think of it as legend, but clairvoyance has revealed that it actually *did* take place."

"There's something about the Flood, however, that people don't realize." An Intense gaze met ours as we sat there in silence, absorbed in this new information and on fire with curiosity.

"What has been recorded as the Great Flood was actually the final inundation of Atlantis."

Our eyes were beaming with fascination. How interesting! The Great Flood caused the final destruction of Atlantis!

Werner leaned back on the front edge of his desk again and continued, "The person we've come to know as Noah was an

Atlantean. Many cultures have recorded accounts of the Flood.
The Babylonian story of Gilgamesh is the most accurate."

And now he returned once again to the enigmatic statement
that began our intriguing lesson.

"We are now living at a time of Noah. We have again come to
the point when there will be major Earth changes taking place.
And it is at this lower left edge of the wheel, just after the Kali
Yuga and the Age of Pisces, when these Earth changes are even
more pronounced than on the other side."

"An event more catastrophic than the Great Flood?" My mind
raced, imagining the possibilities. Some of us glanced at each
other in amazement. Others kept their eyes locked on Werner's.

"However", Werner's voice broke into our raging thoughts, "this
time is different from all the other times that have gone before --
dating back many millions of years into ancient history. This time
will be different. We are living in extraordinary times! Let's take
our break and then come back to discuss this further."

What a moment to pause for a break! At least there seemed
to be a note of optimism. At the same time a strong note of
suspense permeated the room. We were all eager to know
exactly what made our point in time so extraordinary.

3

Extraordinary Times,

Extraordinary Beings

Seats filled again quickly. We were all so eager to hear more of these incredible details. The mood was very different from the silent, solemn atmosphere at the start of the class.

Werner entered the room and a hush swept in after him. With a sense of duty and an upbeat spark of optimism, Werner cleared his throat as he took a seat at his desk. Everyone's gaze met in the depth of Werner's eyes.

"We've been viewing the Wheel of Ages," Werner glanced at the diagram to his right. "We are living in extraordinary times ... and we've all chosen to be here at this point in time."

"As I pointed out earlier, something big will be happening in your lifetimes. We have reached the point in the 25,920 year cycle when major Earth changes will be happening."

The way he put it seemed to indicate this major change would happen after he had passed.

"This 25,920 year cycle is the duration of a larger revolution on a cosmic scale. These times of major transitions have occurred periodically over the life of this planet."

Here Werner took a brief pause. His mood again foreshadowed the importance of his next statement.

"Our point in time is a very unique one. This time -- this period of the Earth changes -- will be different from any of the countless Great Ages that have gone by."

"The change will be entirely different this time. There is a group on a spiritual plane or dimension which will be playing a large part in what is to come. This group is known as the Hierarchy. They are a very real group that has overseen and helped humanity from the beginning."

"Normally, throughout the cycles of time, whenever these cataclysms have occurred most of the Earth's population has been wiped out. The few remaining individuals left to repopulate Earth have had to start over from a much more primitive level.

20

Their histories along with memories or records of their progress and technology have pretty much died with them, living on in some cases only as vague legends."

What came to mind when he said this were the legends of Atlantis and Lemuria, and also of the ancient Greek gods.

"This point in time is very significant, and the change this time will be unlike anything that has happened before. The whole Transition will play out differently this time around. It's very important for some reason for most of humanity to remain alive and make this Transition or transformation consciously. It will be no *ordinary* Transition. This time it will truly be a '*transformation*'."

Such a concept and such a statement! And this was just the beginning! After another brief pause Werner added this statement.

"I used the word 'transformation' because the shift this time will be different from all the previous periods of Transition. All life will transform to a finer level of existence."

Werner cleared his throat again and continued, "Normally the Hierarchy holds meetings twice a century to discuss the progress of humanity. They look at the course humanity and individuals have taken and they decide whether one or more of them is needed to help mankind move forward in one way or another."

"Sometimes it is by influencing someone's thoughts. This happens all the time -- and often people dismiss the thoughts or unfortunately don't act on them. At times these *influences* have greatly helped humanity in the long run and have marked major stepping stones in history."

"Sometimes this influence is more physical. A member of the Hierarchy may come to live on Earth or they may 'overshadow' or bring their thoughts into someone living on Earth. Often at those times religions have grown up around these figures. They have either been members of the Hierarchy or people the Hierarchy has overshadowed with their thoughts, influencing them to write or carry out their work."

"As I said, generally throughout history the Hierarchy has held meetings twice a century. At these meetings the progress and status of humanity is evaluated. In addition they discuss how best to help mankind continue moving past blocks or setbacks -- continuing to move forward on the upward spiral of life and growth."

"The twentieth century, however, brought such a speeded up momentum. This has resulted in many dramatic changes both outwardly as well as inward changes in how people think and act. It has been necessary for the Hierarchy to hold these meetings more often in the twentieth century."

We all sat there amazed. Hard to imagine this vague and illusive entity known as *the Hierarchy* really existed and actually did hold meetings! Again, the best words to describe this are mind-blowing, though I've over-used the words already. Yet, as unreal as it sounded, we all had this deep, gut level sense that all of this was true. Our concepts of the world, life and reality were forever altered that day. The view broadened daily in those fascinating two years of studies.

I can understand how this may be sounding unbelievable, and I hope I haven't lost you. Strange as it may sound, it goes along with what scientists have said. They've come to realize now that life is composed of many different dimensions. This is something that will be more fully understood as time goes on into the future.

Rudolf Steiner was known as a "spiritual scientist" who could see these other dimensions or planes. He was born at a time when his abilities and contributions to humanity were very much needed and he brought a new level of understanding to those who were ready and eager to receive it. Others with this ability of spiritual sight or clairvoyance have verified his findings as accurate.

4

An Otherworldly Event

This enlightening class continued and there was more surprising information to come. It was information that would rearrange our whole concept of life and any thoughts we had about this group known as the Hierarchy.

Werner got up from his desk and came around to the front of it to be closer to us. This created a more conversational, friendly atmosphere. He leaned against the front of the desk and continued.

"At the full moon of June 1945 the Hierarchy held a very significant meeting. The purpose of this particular meeting was to discuss whether or not it would be necessary for the great being known as the Christ to return in a physical body. Or was his closeness to humanity in the etheric realm enough to help with the current crisis facing humanity? He could still make himself available to appear if needed and also to intervene if it became necessary."

There was a gravity to Werner's tone, and I could sense he knew and had personally foreseen just what faces us in the future. He'd never go into very specific details, but he *did* give us an idea of what to expect.

Hearing an actual date of the Hierarchy's meeting had an almost shocking effect. It gave a surreal sense of reality to this whole *otherworldly* event. At the same time it seemed so bizarre -- like such a *physical* thing for such a non-physical entity to do. Our thoughts of what the Hierarchy was, and the reality of this overseeing body, by whatever name one chooses to call it, were forever altered that day.

"Given humanity's current situation with the increasing chaos and unrest and what faces mankind in the future, it was decided *Christ* that Christ indeed would need to return in a physical body. And because of the magnitude of both what is coming and what is needed, forty-two other members of the Hierarchy also made the decision to return in order to support the Christ in the task required to help humanity."

"Although it might sound like a contradiction, incarnating into a physical body for a member of the Hierarchy is very dangerous. These evolved beings emit such Light that they become *danger* immediate targets for forces of darkness on this dense physical level -- targets for lower forces which try to put as many obstacles in their path as they can. This includes wearing them thin with difficulties and hardships. The forces of darkness will do anything to make evolved beings lose sight of their goals and to render them ineffective in completing the task that they had come to do. Even great beings are subject to this once they are living in human bodies in the physical dimension. So it's a very real sacrifice for a great being to actually incarnate into a physical body."

"There *have* been times when, being *at the mercy* of these bombarding negative forces, they have been so overwhelmed with hardships and negativities that these enlightened beings actually regressed. It hasn't happened often, but constant obstacles and temptations have on occasion created karma for these great beings. At times it has taken lifetimes to work this off before reaching back to their natural more perfected state."

"Momentary apparitions or brief manifestations into a body are much easier for members of the Hierarchy to do if their help is needed. And these can be very effective in instigating changes for the better. This time however, Christ along with forty-two other members of the Hierarchy will be incarnating and living among you in physical bodies *in your lifetimes!*"

Wow! This was sounding like science fiction. And yet, there was an underlying unquestionable sense of truth to it all. We sensed and *felt* the reality behind the words Werner spoke, as always.

26

"Christ *will be* returning in your lifetime! And his ancient soul name is Maitreya (my-TRAY'-uh)."

I will never forget this statement. It was extraordinary to hear, and made such an impact on all of us. It's information I have lived with for decades, since the mid '70s. In a way I've felt like an *observer* of events unfolding. This information was kept in mind as I watched events unfold around the world.

I remember in the late '90s when I happened to wake up in the middle of the night and put on the Art Bell radio program. Benjamin Creme was being interviewed that night. He spoke of a Master who was living at that time in England. He was called Maitreya. This fascinated me, and I've been following this ever since.

This is a major event, and something that I want especially to explain. Maitreya *is* the Christ. It is simply the ancient name for the immortal Christ, and He has returned to live among us at this time. He will announce His presence in the near future when the time is right.

I realize that to some this may sound like nonsense or fantasy, while others may have a very unfortunate misunderstanding of the name. It is so unfortunate that some have totally misunderstood the name and have wrongly connected it in their minds with a force of darkness. In their misunderstanding some have gotten worked up and fearful about the name. Fear can be a powerful force, creating or manifesting the very unwanted conditions that one is afraid of. This is what has sometimes happened in the case of some of Benjamin Creme's listeners in the past on CoastToCoastam.com radio programs. Some listeners have gotten themselves so worked up that they actually got sick or created other unwanted conditions by the strength of this misunderstood belief. When one's mind is clouded by fear it acts as a powerful form of visualization, causing unwanted conditions to manifest. This is why it is so important not to allow fear or nervousness to take hold of you. It can stand in the way of hearing and knowing the real *truth*. This holds true for any emotion that we allow to take over and overpower our sense of reason. The power of beliefs is especially potent when it comes to religion and religious beliefs. You can see this in action in certain churches where the congregation becomes very emotionally involved. Emotions can be strong enough to cause certain symptoms or reactions.

It is very important to me to share this broader understanding that the name Maitreya is truly the ancient name used by the Christ. I am hoping this will help to clear up misunderstanding.

Back to the year 1974 -- Werner continued the class with another interesting statement.

"Many of the Masters have been living in secluded monasteries perched in the Himalayan Mountains of Tibet for thousands of years. In the 1800s there were a few people who trekked miles over those mountains to find them. Some wrote of their travels and meetings with the Masters."

28

"Baird T. Spalding was one of them. He wrote of his travels in a series of books called *Life and Teachings of the Masters of the Far East.* Murdo MacDonald-Bayne was another who wrote of his travels and meeting the Masters including Jesus in books called *Beyond The Himalayas* and its sequel *The Yoga Of The Christ,* among many other books."

"Alice A. Bailey was another one. She was born in 1880 and played a key role in providing information from the Masters. There are *many* interesting Bailey books which explain spiritual information in detail. She was in direct contact with the Masters, and her books contain information directly from them. Along with Helena Blavatsky and a few others, Alice Bailey was instrumental in forming Theosophy."

4a Alice A. Bailey.

Werner went on to explain that Theosophy contains the deepest truths of religion. The writings of Theosophy came from people who were in direct contact with Masters. The information is intriguing because it has come directly from the Masters. Rudolf Steiner himself had been a Theosophist. He realized an even deeper level of understanding was needed -- one that would encompass and improve every aspect of human life. Steiner saw the spiritual level behind everything. He wanted to improve our lives through this understanding.

"Rudolf Steiner realized a more scientific approach to spiritual things was necessary during his time. An approach was needed that would also address more practical matters of everyday life. He left the Theosophical Society to bring in other, new information. From the basis of Theosophy, Steiner created Anthroposophy to be the Science of Spirit. It's actually the study of man from the aspect of Spiritual Science."

"From time to time throughout the ages a Master or great Teacher has incarnated into a specific area if it was needed. They usually can't interfere too much with the course of humanity and free will, but they can raise awareness and generate right thinking by setting examples. For so many Masters to incarnate at one time is extremely rare. It makes this point in time unusual and exciting. In fact, when this plan was revealed after their meeting in June 1945 all souls wanted to be on Earth for these events. They wanted to be present and to be a part of this major Transition. The baby boom started in full force to make this possible for souls to begin incarnating in larger numbers."

Baby Boom here when to be Masters start to re incarnate

30

This was all so interesting. I grew up going to Catholic schools, and we always heard of angels and the Hierarchy helping humanity. But, deep down, these words of the nuns and priests never really got across the reality of it in such a vital, present and very real way. This was amazing!

"What about the people who will die before this happens? People are dying every day," a student asked.

Werner's expression was kind but serious. I could tell he wanted to answer all of our questions in the best way he could to help clarify our understanding.

"Some will have time to reincarnate. Others who won't be here in physical bodies will be present on other levels and will participate just as well from whatever level they're on."

Then he touched on a subject I knew was a very sensitive one for Werner. I was about to find out why. I had seen on an earlier occasion how the news of a young person's suicide affected him deeply.

With a somber expression, Werner continued, "Those who commit suicide may miss this one-in-a-million chance their souls had arranged to be here for. It's always sad for me to hear of people who are so overwhelmed with the difficulties of physical life that they see no way out other than to end their lives. They had incarnated at this point in time to be here for this extremely rare event. They may never have a chance like this again -- to be present for the events that are coming."

"But won't they be present on another level, like you said?" someone asked.

"It may not happen like this with suicides. Those souls are met by their guides and go to a place of learning and sort of recovery. They've stunted their growth pattern and have set themselves back by destroying the life they had come to live. They'll have a chance in the future to make up for this life and the lessons they had come to learn, but in many cases they unknowingly ruined this rare opportunity to be present at this point in time. It could be possible they will miss the events that are coming -- even as observers on other levels. We don't know for sure."

"I had mentioned how, from time to time, a member of the Hierarchy incarnates if it is needed. The Second World War posed a particular problem. Conditions then were ripe for many forces of darkness to enter into this physical realm. This happened with Hitler, Mussolini, etc., and all those who surrounded them. It created an urgent need for members of the Hierarchy to incarnate in and around Europe. They needed to come as counterpoints of Light to all the forces of darkness that were flooding in then."

"One of those incarnating members of the Hierarchy was a man named Franz Bardon. I recommend you read the book, *Frabato the Magician*. It's a biography of Franz Bardon's adult

32

life, and tells how he made his living as a stage magician. He chose the stage name Frabato because in a previous life he had a similar name."

4b Franz Bardon.

Etheric plane over Gobi Desert

"Franz Bardon's life was truly amazing. The book is astounding, and describes some of his performances. He had enormous abilities and would actually manifest items as well as people. There is also a drawing in this book of the actual building where the Hierarchy holds its meetings. They meet on the etheric plane actually suspended above the Earth. The physical location is hovering in the etheric plane above the Gobi desert. In a finer plane or dimension they create a temple-like building each time they have one of these meetings. It's an interesting structure with very specific designs. You'll see in the illustration in this book how the building is ornately decorated. The interesting aspect of the

33

many designs on the building is that each symbol represents a different Age and culture on Earth."

Book

"This temple or meeting place is called Shamballa and the book "Shangri-la" was written based on legends of Shamballa."

Werner was right! The book *Frabato the Magician* is fascinating. And I've meticulously studied each decoration and symbol on that drawing of Shamballa -- trying to get a sense of what age and culture each symbol represents. It's intriguing! Bardon's life was remarkable, and seems to mirror many of the scenes in the film *The Illusionist,* although the film's setting was an earlier war. I've wondered if the film was inspired by Bardon's book. It seems like such a close match. Bardon ended up having to run for his life. The Nazi's saw his power, and when he refused to join them they finally caught and imprisoned Bardon. The book ends with his imprisonment. Privately I've imagined him dematerializing from his cell. What a shock *that* would have been if it indeed happened that way!

Werner continued, "In the book, *Frabato the Magician*, it is explained that when Franz was notified about a meeting of the Hierarchy, he would lay down and go out-of-body to these meetings while his body lay 'sleeping' in his European home. There is also another interesting short biography about him called *Memories of Franz Bardon*. It was written by his son and gives the perspective of having this extraordinary person as a father. He describes what it was like growing up with a father who could do things such as manifesting objects etc."

34

"Getting back to the Christ, when the ancient prophets wrote of him 'coming in the clouds' it was a misunderstanding of what they were seeing. They described their visions in the best way they could at the time, because they couldn't understand modern technology. Many of these Masters, as I said, have stayed with the Earth and have been living in monasteries in the Himalayan Mountains. What the prophets were seeing when they wrote of him 'coming in the clouds' was actually him coming down from Lhasa, Tibet by airplane."

"Christ-Maitreya, along with other members of the Hierarchy will be living among you, unknown, in ordinary looking human bodies. Some may be writing books and others may be organizing events etc. They'll be working in any way they can to help people grow in awareness and understanding. Some may be acting totally behind the scenes and not outwardly visible at all. Their task is to reach and awaken as many people as they can, to whatever extent they can, before this big change occurs."

"In order to make this Transition consciously it will be necessary for an increased level of awareness among humanity and also for an increased frequency level of energy to be sent streaming to Earth. This is necessary both for the survival of individual people as well as for the planet itself to have the elevated energy levels to be able to make it through this major Transition that is coming in the near future."

"In the past at each of these points of catastrophe most of Earth's population has passed and cities have been destroyed. The relatively few surviving ones would have to begin civilization again. These cycles have gone on this way for ages. It's been a gradually ascending cycle. Over and over civilization would begin again on a more primitive level each time until eventually it would catch up and go beyond where they had been before the last catastrophe. This time the Transition will be different than all others in the past."

Again Werner was silent for a few moments while we contemplated all this new information. It was really rearranging all of our concepts of life and beings on spiritual dimensions.

Then someone asked, "Do we know when this will happen? When will Christ and the Masters be coming down from Tibet?"

"No one knows the exact date but it will be soon ... in your lifetimes. Some think this has already begun and that they have started coming down from Tibet. Some are now living among us in different countries."

Another voice asked, "Does anyone know where Christ will go? Or where he'll live?"

"No", Werner responded.

"Will He be in a Middle-Eastern body?" another student asked.

"No one knows, but probably. And there again it's also possible for these beings, even after they're here in a body, to temporarily manifest in whatever body they choose. For example they might appear as a beggar, a businessman or an old woman to blend in wherever needed on the spot. Once they're here, they may not always even look the same."

something to Ponder

After a few moments Werner added with a smile and a twinkle in his eyes, "It kind of gives a new meaning to the phrase 'angels unawares.'"

I found the quote he was referring to: "Do not forget to entertain strangers, for in so doing some people have entertained angels unawares." Hebrews 13:2.

How true! I sat there thinking of what an exciting time this is to be alive.

In the early 1980s I was living in Aspen, Colorado. At a Library book sale there I found an intriguing old set of leather-bound books called Life and Teachings of the Masters of the Far East by Baird T. Spalding. I later read that those books find their way to people who have known the Masers. If you have them, you've known the Masters in previous lives. A few years after getting the books they were stolen. Decades later, in May of 2008, I happened to be talking to a friend, Cheryl, about the Masters. I said there were people who hiked across the Himalayan Mountains to meet then in the 1800s, and I told her about Baird T. Spalding's books which I no longer had.

"I wish I still had those books!" I said. "I'd like to read them again!" And I sat there wishing I still had them.

A few days later I was driving south on a highway with my friend Susan. It had just let up raining, and suddenly there was the MOST astounding neon-bright rainbow on the left (east) side of the road opposite our car as we drove south. It was the most *magnificent* rainbow we had ever seen! The band of it was *SO vivid* and *wide* that the orange side went all the way into reds, magenta and violet. And the green side went all the way into blue, blue-violet and then violet! It was incredible! I just kept staring at it saying, "I can't *believe* it! It looks like an illustration in a children's book!" We thought for sure we would see it on the evening news and in the paper the following day.

When we turned east was when the whole episode really got amazing. Now that magnificent rainbow was going across the highway. One end of it was on our right, and the other end was on our left! We seemed to drive right through it, when suddenly the sky lightened up and it was GONE! We had been so mesmerized with this other-worldly rainbow that it was only then this occurred to us. We realized that this magnificent sight had been beside our car for over an hour! Later we were shocked to find nothing about it on the news or in the paper. I couldn't help but wonder if anyone else saw it.

The next day, while walking my dog in front of the library, I saw they were having a book sale. I hadn't been to one in a while, not wanting to spend money. This particular day, however, I *knew* that I *had* to go. There was something there *for me*. So I went back when the library opened and was drawn to go directly to a certain table to discover a complete, new five-piece set of *Life and Teachings of the Masters of the Far East!* The serendipity left me almost stunned, and I walked home lost in a reverie of the past few days.

"Were those books donated a few days ago prompted by our conversation and my wishing for them?" I thought. "Or did I bring them up in the first place because I subconsciously sensed they were there at the library next door?"

The thoughts kept running through my head -- of that unusual weekend. It seemed like the rainbow was somehow connected to the books. And then I realized! It was the Wesak Festival *Look* weekend! Wesak is the most sacred time of the year to the Theosophists, Anthroposophists, Hindus and Buddhists. It's one of the Spring Full Moon Festivals when the Masters come closest to the Earth and humanity. It was such a strange and interesting series of events to have happened then.

5

Another Class

Revelations Continue

The room seemed to vibrate with a sense of excitement the following day. All eyes were on Werner as we sat waiting for him to begin -- wondering what more could possibly be added to the mind blowing scenario of the day before. The statement that Christ will be returning in our lifetimes and his ancient soul name is Maitreya was surprising enough all by itself! Werner leaned against the front of his desk and smiled.

"Just to review a little bit, we've been discussing this point in time and some of the features that make it unique. We saw that our point in time is a period of great Transition. The 25,920 year Wheel of Ages is a gradual progression of three steps forward, one or two steps back in an ever-ascending spiral."

"Again, just to review a little, this time around the Transition will be different from all previous ones. It will be more profound this time. One other very significant aspect of it is this. It is very important this time that most of humanity makes this transition alive and conscious, without dying and having to be reborn to start building society over from a more primitive level. Most significantly perhaps is the fact that the Christ along with forty-two other Masters will be very involved in what will be taking place this time around. They will be working behind the scenes to ensure that the greatest amount of the Earth's population will be able to make this Transition alive and conscious. This time it won't just be reaching another milestone in awareness. The Transition this time will be much greater."

"Over the next few decades elevated energies will be directed toward Earth. It is necessary. The frequencies must be elevated so that humanity and Earth will be able to withstand what is coming. In order to make it through this immense Transition frequencies need to be elevated."

"There will be segments of society who won't be able to handle this increased energy. You will see behaviors getting more and more erratic as we get closer to the twenty-first century and beyond. Despite how it may look from the vantage point of certain erratic segments of society, the energy increase is exceedingly important. It is necessary for both the planet and individuals in order for this Transition to happen. Along with heightened energies being sent to Earth, there will be many other efforts to raise awareness. Groups and movements will form and books will be written etc. to raise awareness."

41

"What the Masters have chosen will not be easy, and there will come a time when Christ and other Masters will need to make themselves known. This will definitely *not* be an easy task because, for one thing, society has perhaps never been so analytical and hard to convince of anything. It was difficult enough two thousand years ago to convince people of Christ's identity. Can you imagine how difficult it will be now when the time comes?" *S. M.*

Werner's expression looked serious, but it lightened a bit as he started to explain something else to us.

"Christ, who is also known by the ancient name of Maitreya, will begin to make his presence known in an interesting way. He won't, in all likelihood, be using either of those names. This may sound surprising, but it's very likely He will be making use of current technology. When the time comes to start appearing publicly it will be gradually through the media. In other words, it will begin on the public scene with television interviews. The times call for it to be handled very carefully." A hand went up, breaking the trancelike state we were in.

"Any ideas what programs he may be on?" a student asked.

"No. No one knows."

Thoughts raced through my mind like raindrops in a torrent. So the time has finally come. The events that have been

42

prophesied for millennia will be happening in our lifetime! We will be able to witness it all. And it will begin in the current technology of the times ... bizarre to imagine. Christ, and forty-two other Masters, will be living among us as regular people! We truly _are_ living at the most extraordinary time! And this coming Transition will be a very positive one.

There's something else that comes to mind when I think of Werner and my time at the Institute. One day I asked him why he had chosen Detroit, of all places, for his Waldorf Teacher Training center. His answer was, "I was guided to start it here because there were certain souls I had been wanting to who would come to this location."

I've thought of that statement over the years. I'm glad to have been among those souls who studied with Werner Glas and our other wonderful professor, Hans Gebert, at the Waldorf Teacher Training Institute of Detroit. I'm also glad to have met such a wonderful group of fellow students there.

There is another unforgettable memory that comes to mind as I sit here. It was an incident that shows Werner's unusual abilities as well as his flare for drama. One day we were all seated in class waiting for Werner to arrive. He lived only a few blocks away, and always walked to class. Actually Werner didn't drive. He shared with me that his extreme ability to see other levels would have made it very unsafe for him to drive.

This particular day we were all seated at the tables when suddenly Werner burst into the classroom looking all disheveled and totally out of breath. It was such a sight!

"I just escaped from a group of thugs who were about to attack me!" he panted to his desk and with a great sense of relief fell into his seat.

"I heard them coming up behind me and knew what they were about to do. So I shot around to face them, summoning the greatest power of visualization I could create. With a sudden force I raised my arm on high as if I had a huge sword in my hand and shouted with all my might. Those kids froze in a state of shock. They were terrified and ran away as fast as they could. And I ran just as fast in the other direction!" He kind of chuckled at the image of it all.

We sat there captivated by this emotional scene. It was a sight we could imagine so vividly. Werner in his long black cape-like overcoat and his almost mideval presence would carry out those actions so perfectly -- raising his arm with a terrifying force, and his deep resounding voice would unleash a thunderous shout!

"Did that sword actually manifest?!" I was so lost in the account and the visualization that I could "see" it there so clearly! I guess we had all been wondering the same thing. If anyone could manifest a vision in an extreme circumstance, it would certainly be Werner!

"Did they see the sword in your hand?"

"I'm not sure," Werner answered, still catching his breath. "I think they very well may have seen it. It was certainly real for me!"

These were just a few of the classes and incidents over that two-year period. Each and every class brought amazing discoveries. The Waldorf Teacher Training Institute moved to Spring Valley, New York in 1986 and became Sunbridge College. Werner passed in October of 1991. In 2010 Sunbridge College became Sunbridge Institute as a tribute to its roots at the Waldorf Teacher Training Institute of Detroit. It continues to be a center for higher learning in the deepest sense of the words, offering courses in a wide range of subjects from a profoundly deep perspective.

Please visit Sunbridge.edu to read the interesting biographical tribute to Werner Glas. It's a little hidden on the site. To find it click on "About Sunbridge" in the bar at the upper right. From there click "History of Sunbridge" in the left column. After reading that page for a short version on how Werner started the Institute, click "Biography of Werner Glas" which appears below the "History of Sunbridge" link when you click on it.

The biography gives a short and very interesting synopsis of Werner's life from childhood on. His life was quite a journey! Synchronicity was very evident, leading him through a sort of perilous maze in childhoow to a safe harbor. From there he was directed in the course of his life as Waldorf educator.

6

Exploring

a Multi-Faceted Universe

The wealth of information gained over those two years of studies brought tremendous insight. It gave answers to the deepest questions I would often wonder about throughout my life. We explored the very meaning and purpose of life, along with many other topics that had once only been mysteries.

Werner affirmed the reality of life on other planets and the fact that Earth has been visited by other-worldly (extraterrestrial) races dating back into the ancient past. One particular statement fascinated me.

"There is life on every planet and many of the moons in our Solar System. They are all lush and green on other planes otherwise known as dimensions)", he explained.

The statement was absolutely fascinating to me. Again, this was back in the mid-70s. It was the first time I had heard of other dimensions of existence. I had read about other "planes" in metaphysical books, but thought of it more as the one spiritual, after-life, realm. The idea that there were many different planes or *dimensions* was so interesting. Celestial bodies which appear to be totally lifeless, from our very limited perspective on this dense physical plane, could be filled with life on a totally different *dimension*! Our perspective from this dense physical plane is a very one-sided view. The universe is actually made up of a multitude of different dimensions. This is an important feature that must be taken into account in order to fully understand the deepest levels of life and the universe.

Werner explained that the Egyptian gods were called Syrian gods because they were from Sirius. The spelling of that title was translated from Heiroglyphics as *Syrian* with a *y*, so it is sometimes assumed they had some kind of association with Syria. The true meaning of the phrase "Syrian god" was because they were advanced "godlike" beings from Sirius. He explained that the deep connection with Sirius can be seen in the very names Isis and Osiris. They were both from Sirius, and their names very specifically reflect their origin.

This becomes even more intriguing when we look at the Dogon tribe, also from the African continent. Their details of gods visiting from SIrius are amazing. They knew about Sirius B before it was discovered. They even drew star maps on their cave walls showing Sirius A and B long before scientists even knew about them.

Sirius

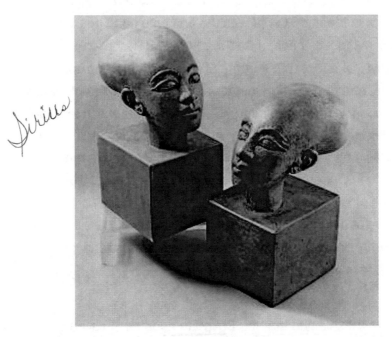

6a Akhenaten's daughters. Busts from the Cairo Museum.

In our discussion about Isis and Osiris one of their unique traits was brought up. They all had unusually elongated skulls. Much later, at the time of the 18th dynasty, Akhenaten and his entire family were also known to have long skulls. This included Nefertiti, who was a wife of Akhenaten.

In the following years, when I'd see documentaries of African tribes who bind their children's skulls to elongate them, this class came to mind. I realized that the ancient memory of those "gods" who had visited their continent in much earlier times was kept alive through the generations. It seems the African people tried to copy the traits of those "gods", evidently to make themselves more worthy or *godlike*.

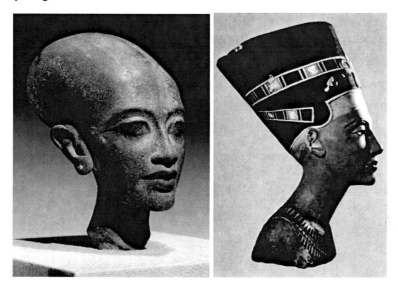

6b On the left is a bust that I believe depicts Nefertiti. The long skull gives a new understanding her headdress seen in 6c

When I went to Egypt in November of both 1997 and 1999, the perspective gained at the Waldorf Institute gave me a deeper understanding of things I saw there. Another intriguing feature of Akhenaton's family was large ears. Interestingly, Werner studied ears and earlobes, though he never fully explained what the different types of ears indicated to him.

I have to show you what I found in the Coptic temple behind the worker's village at Deir el-Medina. Deir el-Medina is the village where those who worked on the Valley of the Kings lived. In the Coptic temple behind the worker's village there is one particular room that clearly had a very special purpose. It is a small, narrow room with highly decorated walls. The Syrian gods are shown on the left wall with red balls above their heads, as they very often are shown. This feature seems to indicate a special sacredness. I found it to be an intriguing clue to their extra-planetary origin. To me the red balls could indicate vehicles that had brought those Syrian gods to Earth. I'm sure those vehicles would have seemed sacred to the ancient people, who would have seen them as *"Chariots of the Gods"*.*

6d Syrian gods on a temple wall at Deir el-Medina.

Most interesting to me was the wall facing this one of the gods. It is really astonishing! Facing this wall is a huge mural of a vehicle. First of all, I've never seen anything else in Egypt done in such a large mural-like size. In this image, a canoe was used to *clearly indicate* a *vehicle*. It is, however, not just any vehicle. The canoe has a large dome above it, and resting on top of that dome

* *Chariots of the Gods*, by Zecharia Sitcin

is the red ball which is often above the heads of the Syrian gods.

6e "Boat of Sokar" Egyptian vehicle. Shown in color at ExploringSacredSpace.com *Website*

The canoe has an exaggerated curved, unlike any other canoes or canoe images I've seen in Egypt. Its paddles are resting in the holders at the left end. To me this seems to indicate that it did not need the paddles to travel. More indications of this are the blue colored birds along the upper right edge of the canoe. A large wing-like flap also hangs from the right end. Both images symbolize flight. The blue-green birds can be seen much more clearly in color on the site listed above. Some final very significant features of this vehicle are the tripod legs resting on a platform. I was told by an Egyptian researcher that this is known as the "Boat of Sokar", but no one knows exactly what it was.

One of the most fascinating of the Egyptian gods is Ptah.

6f Ptah, the Egyptian god with gray skin and a bodysuit.

He is one of the most ancient and highly revered of the gods who was known to be extremely wise and knowledgeable. Intriguingly, unlike all other Egyptian figures, Ptah is always shown in a one-piece white body suit. His skin is gray or sometimes blue-gray, and he is shown with a little tank on his back. This mysterious little tank is often connected to Ptah's mouth with a tube. He is also most often shown with no hair.

There is another important figure who supports the idea that these advanced beings they called "gods" were races from other planets outside of Earth. This was a highly revered god known as Hathor. She is a very interesting individual with strikingly different ears, and was just one of an entire race known among certain Mid-Eastern and Asian cultures as the Hathors. *Big ears below)*

6g The god Hathor.

53

The ancient Egyptians saw her ears as somehow related to a
cow. In fact she is most often shown with the arched horns of a
bull above her head. Inside these bull horns is the red disk which
I feel represents the sacred vehicle of these gods.

And here is an image of Hathor inside her sacred vehicle. She
even has what seems to be a control of some sort in her hands.
You can see the bull's horns above her head with the red disk
inside them. If you to go to ExploringSacresSpace.com, and click
on Chapters + Illustrations you'll see these images in color.

6h Hathor inside her sacred vehicle.

To the right of Hathor is another intriguing image which to
some scientists suggest that the ancient Egyptians created simple
batteries and light bulbs, probably using vinegar as a battery acid.
Here we see an image coming out of a vase or vial with a red rim

implying that it is lit up. Just as I believe the red circles above the heads are indications of these balls glowing. UFOs have been seen and documented glowing red. The ancient light bulb theory was tested by scientists on the National Geographic channel. They used vinegar to recreate this image shown on Egyptian walls. And they *did* light up! Below is another image I had taken in a very special lower room at the Dendera temple. These glowing objects would have been seen as "magic" to the ancient Egyptians. And thus they related these objects to the gods.

6i Image from a lower room in the Hathor temple at Dendera .

The serpent within these light bulb images implies the kundalini power of awakened energy which is often shown at the third eye on headdresses of the pharoahs. The bulb on the left is held up by a god figure with the red disk above her head. The bulb on the right is held by the sacred djed stone. Interestingly the figure in front of this djed stone could be seen as wearing a helmet and mask. I believe that the origin of certain cultures venerating cows and bulls goes back to the Hathors, which became known as an entire race of exalted beings.

Another god who attracts my attention is Thoth. Interestingly, Edgar Cayce said that Thoth was an earlier lifetime of Jesus.

6j Thoth, shown with a quill, taught Egyptians to write. Known as a god of great wisdom and a counselor of pharaohs.

Werner had spoken quite a bit about Edgar Cayce. He verified that Cayce had been Ra in a previous Egyptian life, and that the information given in his readings is accurate and true. The Cayce readings often clarify and give a better understanding of the distant past. The Cayce Association for Research and Enlightenment (ARE) has a compilation of everything Cayce said dealing with Egypt. It is a hard-bound two-volume set called *Egypt, Parts I and II.* I'm glad to have this set in my collection of books.

No one knows exactly why the ibis bird is associated with Thoth, but it was his totem-like emblem. He is often shown with the head of an ibis. Sometimes his skin is also shown as the same gray or blue-gray color seen in images of Ptah.

6k Ptah on the left. 6l Thoth with an arc and disk on his head

On square columns in 6k, to the right of Ptah, other gods are shown with the red ball above their heads. Ptah is on the far left edge. In 6l on the right Thoth has the red ball above his head, which could be interpreted as resting inside of a canoe with an exaggerated curve.

Thoth is holding the sacred Ankh in his right hand and one of the sacred rods in the other. Gregg Braden thinks this rod may have been used to vibrationally attune the brain. He thought someone would possibly strike it like a tuning fork and then hold it along the back of the head, which would be why it had that specific angle. The Ankh cross is also called the "key of life", and there are many interpretations of its possible uses. Many people currently believe it was used for vibrational work.

I recently met Michael Tellinger who has done interesting archaeological research around the world. Michael thinks the Ankh was used as a tuning fork for both healing people and bringing them to life. He feels that each ankh would need to be calibrated to one's own body energy. Michael has done extensive research in his quest to discover the ancient origins of mankind. See the Books and Recommendations page. Both *Adam's Calendar* and *Temples of the African gods* by Tellinger are filled with images showing large circular stone walls. There are hundreds of these throughout Africa. Michael's research indicates these highly detailed patterns of stone circles were used to create sound or saser (sound) frequencies. Interestingly, he said GPS tracking systems don't function above these stone circles which he believes resonate to a certain sound or saser frequency.

There was one other fascinating Egyptian artifact that stands out in my mind. It is a very unique item in the Cairo Museum that doesn't fit in with traditional archaeology. Sometimes it is stored out of sight in their basement and not even put on display, as it doesn't fit into traditional archaeology. We were fortunate to find it on display in one of the rooms on the museum's second floor in 1999.

6m The mysterious curved disk in the Cairo Museum.

This peculiar wheel-like artifact has a very modern look although it is ancient. The openings in the center of this curved disk seem clear indications of an axel or rod being used. Notice the raised areas on the left and right that curve in toward the center. They are a very aerodynamic feature, and show that this disk was designed for a very specific purpose. Gregg Braden had taken us to see this wheel. As we stood looking at it, I could *see* it in use in ancient times. I *saw* it spinning very rapidly on a rod. The spinning created an extremely high-pitched tone, which I could also *hear*. Gregg then explained this exact concept. He also felt it was placed on a rod and spun at a rate of speed to create a high vibrational pitch.

This is another one of those ancient and very mysterious artifacts that don't fit into the traditional view of Egyptian archaeology. It's one more clue in support of ancient technologies such as saser frequency used in the ancient past.

Another very intriguing artifact are the intricate Flower of Life images found inscribed into the granite Osirian walls. The Osirian was still being excavated behind the temple of Seti at Abydos. It is below ground level, and is often filled with flood water.

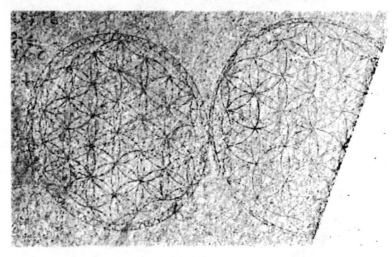

6n Flower of Life images inscribed in the Osirian.

The Osirian dates much further back into antiquity than the Seti I temple in front of it, which is one of the most ancient Egyptian temples. .

The precision of these Flower of Life patterns makes them all the more intriguing. They appear to have been laser-etched into the granite. Again this seems to indicate technologies far more advanced than what is traditionally accepted.

This Flower of Life pattern can be found in places around the world. Visit www.world-mysteries.com/sar_sage1.htm for more details. Leonardo da Vinci also studied the Flower of Life pattern. He had a strong interest in in both the Platonic Solids and figures of Sacred Geometry. Werner explained that Leonardo had been a great Initiate, and he had also been one of the central figures around Jesus.

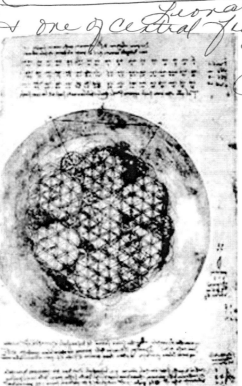

6o A page from Leonardo's notes.

This Flower of Life pattern is considered to be a pattern of "sacred geometry" which was the initial form that all life grew from. The forms of sacred geometry, which include the Platonic Solids, are forms whose properties explain deeper aspects and secrets of reality. For example, its pattern is formed with twelve circles around a central one.

This forms the sacred twelve plus the one central figure, making thirteen. The Flower of Life pattern is considered to contain secrets about the very beginnings of life in the Universe.

6p Flower of Life: twelve circles surrounding a thirteenth.

One other mysterious image is found on an upper wall of the the ancient Seti temple at Abydos. It depicts vehicles from thousands of years in the future from that time period. This image is an enigma that has been studied by people around the world.

Some wonder if it is a prophecy indicating a unique significance to our point in time.

6q Mysterious wall of futuristic vehicles in the Seti temple at Abydos.

More indications supporting a multi-faceted universe came from my classes at the Waldorf Institute. Werner explained that every planet, as well as many of the moons in our solar system, have abundant life on other planes or dimensions. I mention this and explain this further in chapter nine. The dimension we live on is one of the lower ones. We enter a finer dimension when we die, and also every night during sleep. He encouraged us to write down our dreams when we wake up in the morning before our feet touch the ground. This is when the mind is able to recall dream details most clearly. "Dream life", as Werner called it, is a very significant portion of one's total existence. Often important lessons and examples are given at this time. The subconscious mind often twists the images and circumstances in dreams, making them seem surreal. In time, however, if dreams are recorded the mind can be trained to have a clearer memory of what actually happened and the lessons that were taught. It is a way of learning from those other dimensions or planes of existence.

63

Another subject of particular interest to Werner was Saint Francis and the significance of that whole episode in history. Saint Francis had been born in 1181. It was a time of chivalry, troubadours and knights. He was born in the hill town of Assisi, Italy and was called Francesco Bernardone, although his baptismal name was actually John (spelled Gian in Italian). It is believed he was called Francesco (Francis) because his father often traveled to France on business. His father had, in fact, been away in France when Saint Francis was born.

Werner spoke of the significance of both Francis and Claire as souls. Claire was Francis' girlfriend who became a nun when he formed his religious order. The strongest memory I have about that class was Werner talking of his visit to the Assisi church. He had introduced himself to some of the monks there, saying he was an Anthroposophist who had also studied Theosophy. The monks of Assisi were surprisingly familiar with both. They took Werner to their private library where he was surprised to see many books by Rudolf Steiner. The monks and Werner had an interesting discussion on the Spiritual Sciences. It was amazing to hear Werner tell the story himself. It definitely affirmed that some religious groups know more than they will acknowledge publicly.

Werner said there were other religious groups, including the Vatican itself, who also privately recognized and studied Rudolf Steiner's findings. These groups have studied Anthroposophy and they understand and accept Steiner's concepts yet they would never acknowledge this publicly. We asked why they were so secretive about this knowledge, despite their interest in these deeper realities of spirituality. Why wouldn't they publicly announce the truth about these deep facets of existence? It was clearly fascinating to us; the inquisitive twenty-somethings of the mid-'70s. We were totally captivated by this information.

Werner answered that it was kept secret out of fear, control, and their combination. Religions are such tradition, and they're also big business. Much of the world's population doesn't want to accept or even think about these deeper aspects of life. They prefer the simpler traditional explanations for everything.

When I was in Italy in 1974 just before attending the Waldorf Institute, Florence itself was *so* familiar to me. There were instances when timelines seemed to overlap. I would get clear memories of having lived there before. They were as clear, vivid and detailed as memories from years earlier. Some of these memories were in Florence where, for a few moments, my whole consciousness seemed to revert to a time when I had lived there in the 1500s. I *knew* where I had lived and knew the whole area well. I also got glimpses of exactly how the city looked back then.

I want to mention something else stressed very strongly back then. This was considered so crucial we were encouraged to bring it up when interviewing for new students. Fluoride had recently been added to both tap water and toothpaste, with the assertion it is essential for bone strength. Independent research has disputed this however, revealing the opposite longterm effects. From a spiritual/Waldorf perspective, fluoride is a horrible detriment and a symptom of forces counteractive to spiritual growth expanding their influence. Besides contributing to later

65

physical difficulties, perhaps more importantly, fluoride is a significant obstacle to finer soul and spiritual levels of development. A strong effect is disabling the *will* or one's desire to be active. In simple terms, it's been a significant factor in "dumbing down" society as well as making "couch potatoes" out of people, it was explained. An interesting observation is the fluoride campaign began after young people began protesting against ideas such as war and political policies they recognized as unfair.

Another literally "breathtaking" experience happened when we visited Assisi. As our bus rounded the mountain, and the lovely Church of Saint Francis was suddenly straight ahead, part of me literally froze. For a few endless moments I couldn't even breathe. The wind was literally knocked out of me.

6r The church of Saint Francis of Assisi.

Part of me seemed "transported" to that earlier time. I clearly remembered living there before. Many of us have. No wonder the Assisi episode resonates so deeply with many people today. It was another episode in the history of mankind where a breakthrough in awareness occurred. Many of us were present for it. The souls who are at the forefront of the "new age" have often incarnated in groups when these leaps in awareness occur.

I lived, studied and worked in Florence during the spring and summer of 1974. That fall I began my studies at the Waldorf Teacher Training Institute. The experience of having just been in Florence was an amazing bonus for me at the Institute. Studying history and the Renaissance had a much deeper meaning to me. We learned about people whose lives and artwork I had gotten to know so well while living in Florence just a few months earlier.

Werner had quite a bit to say about the artists of the Renaissance. I found it so interesting that Rudolf Steiner could clairvoyantly see previous lives of Renaissance artists. He saw that they had been close to Jesus. Some had even been apostles, which explains all the paintings of the Holy Family.

The cycles that we as souls travel in is certainly a fascinating topic. Time and time again the same groups of souls come at key episodes throughout history. And, as we learned in those classes, it is the same group of souls who come to help usher in new ways of thinking and new episodes in mankind's evolutionary journey of awakening.

7

The Teaching Unfolds

I wanted to explain a little bit about Theosophy, what it is and why it was developed. It has been said Theosophy is not *a* religion, but rather it is *the* religion. It gives a wonderful understanding of religion as a science, minus the egos and dogmas put on it by different religious groups and those who have started various religions.

Most significantly, Theosophical teachings give the best explanation for what spirit and spirituality are at the deepest levels. These are the teachings that have come from the Masters. There's a small booklet which helps to explain Theosophy at a very basic level called *"The Ageless Wisdom Teaching: An Introduction to Humanity's Spiritual Legacy"*, by Benjamin Creme. The Ageless Wisdom teachings are writings by someone who was in conscious contact with the Masters. These include Helena Blavatsky, Alice Bailey, Helena Roerich and Benjamin Creme.

Their writings are *from* the Masters, who wrote *through* these individuals, and I have found them to be fascinating.

Just to give a brief explanation, the Masters are souls who have evolved beyond where humanity on Earth is now. A group of them has remained with the Earth, guiding and helping humanity. These Masters have communicated with the major founders of Theosophy, giving information which these authors wrote as the major Theosophical books.

The purpose of life is the evolution and growth of consciousness. The Masters who have stayed with Earth have been guiding humanity throughout the ages. Theosophy is the teachings these Masters have given through its major founders. The Theosophical books have come out in phases over time. Each phase was designed for the time it was written, becoming successively more suited to each age. With each phase the books were written in a more readable and understandable way for the times.

This Theosophical knowledge has been around for ages, but in the past it was kept secret and known only to those with the correct level of understanding. In current times all of this wisdom has now been made available to anyone.

The words *esoteric* and *occult* both simply mean "hidden", although they still have a negative connotation among people who misunderstand them. The words both refer to knowledge that was previously hidden from the public because in the past it would not have been understood by most people. Especially in the last one hundred years, there has been quickening on all levels. This information is now available to everyone and is being made public to increase the knowledge, understanding and awakening of mankind.

Theosophy began with Helena Petrovna Blavatsky and a few others. Between 1875 and 1890, H.P.B. wrote *The Secret Doctrine* and *Isis Unveiled.* They are each two large volume sets of books. They're the initial or *preparatory phase* of the teaching.

The intermediate phase of the Theosophical teachings came through Annie Besant. She was the second president of the Theosophical Society in India from 1907 until her death in 1933 and she wrote *The Ancient Wisdom, Esoteric Christianity,* and *The Masters,* among other books. She had also recognized the great wisdom in Krishnamurti. Annie Besant encouraged and sponsored Krishnamurti, sending him to England to be educated.

The next phase of the Theosophical teaching was given through an English disciple named Alice A. Bailey between 1919 and 1949. The information in her books was given to her by the Tibetan Master Djwhal Khul. There are many Alice Bailey books, all of which give wonderful information. They are not easy reading, but they're well worth the effort, if only to use for reference.

A large contribution of Alice Bailey was her explanation of the seven rays. These are fundamental energies behind all life in the universe. Each of us has different rays, in various combinations and intensity. Understanding them helps us know what we have to deal with in our lives. In this way we can progress more quickly in our own personal growth.

She also explained what she called the "glamours" of each ray. Those are the lower energy aspects appealing to the ego of each particular ray. Bottom line is that the ego is what slows our individual growth or evolution. Knowing details of the rays helps us understand our natures and also what weaknesses we're vulnerable to on our path through life. This is explained in her book *The Rays and the Initiates Vol. I, Esoteric* Psychology. Here's a brief outline of the rays and a few of their corresponding aspects.

7a Graph of the Rays

Ray	Color	Chakra/Gonad
1st -Will - Power	Red	Crown/Pineal
2nd-Love - Wisdom	Indigo	Heart/Thymus
3rd -Active Intelligence	Green	Throat/Thyroid
4th -Harmony through Conflict	Yellow	Base/Adrenals
5th -Concrete Knowledge	Orange	3rd Eye (Ajna)/Pituitary
6th -Abstract Idealism	Sky Blue	Solar Plexus/Pancreas
7th -Ceremonial Order	Violet	Sacral Center/Gonads

Another lead source of the Theosophical teachings was a Russian disciple named Helena Roerich. The books are called the *Agni Yoga Teachings.* These were given by Helena Roerich between 1924 and 1939. She is particularly intriguing to me. I love reading any of the Agni Yoga teachings because, as an intuitive person, I can *feel* the evolved beings known as the Masters speaking *through* them.

There's a very interesting story behind Helena Roerich. Both she and her gifted artist husband Nicholas were very spiritual and intuitive people. They moved to the United States in 1920, and Helena became a close confidant to President Roosevelt. She delivered information to Roosevelt from the Masters and also gave him medicine which kept him alive almost until the end of WWII. Records in the Library of Congress refer to their correspondence as "the Guru Letters", which were both from the Masters and Helena.

At the time they came to the United States, the Department of Agriculture was actively seeking help to resolve the dust bowl conditions which had devastated a large section of the country. Growing crops there became impossible. Nicholas Roerich had devised a method for making those lands fertile again by using drought-resistant seeds he had found on a trip to China. His plans were being considered and were about to be implemented.

Unfortunately, Roosevelt's political opponent had released information about Helena Roerich being Roosevelt's "guru". This caused a great scandal and uproar. After that Nicholas was no longer consulted for his agricultural ideas and his ingenious plan for making the dust bowl fertile was never implemented. The Roerichs ended up returning to Russia. It was one of those sad moments in history. Nicholas Roerich was another great thinker

72

who, like Nicola Tesla, could have brought such benefit to humanity, alleviating many detrimental conditions if only their ideas had been used. (The Guru Letters are on display at the Roosevelt Museum in Hyde Park, NY.)

Rudolf Steiner also played a part in this whole episode. He was born in Austria in 1861 and died in 1925. Steiner recognized that Theosophy was the true and accurate spiritual information at its deepest levels. He was a Theosophist himself and saw that it could be expanded upon to include systems of education, agriculture, art, dance and medicine.

These new methods created better and healthier conditions for individuals and humanity as a whole. In striving to integrate the knowledge of spirit into all human endeavors, Rudolf Steiner expanded upon Theosophy, creating Anthroposophy. It combines the study of spirit with the needs and conditions of humanity. He was a man very much ahead of his time.

8

Days of Merlin and Arthur

Pivotal Moment in Time

If I single out just one more powerful class, it would be this one ... although truthfully all of the classes resonated with me deeply in one way or another. This is a deeply touching subject for most of us who are at the forefront of the incoming ages and energies. It is the whole episode of King Arthur, Merlin, all the knights, ladies and men of that time and place.

Werner explained that the Hierarchy is needed from time to time to help humanity evolve and move forward. Often at those times one or more of them incarnate to be part of the "drama" that triggers and awakens the new energies. This is what happened, Werner explained, with the whole "drama" of King Arthur.

Werner called these episodes throughout history "dramas". They are the pivotal moments when mankind is helped to awaken in one way or another, crossing over a new threshold in awareness. They are the episodes in mankind's growth when a new quality of consciousness is achieved.

Just as an aside, one particular class comes to mind as I write this. We broke up into groups and were assigned to act out a significant drama in the history of humanity. Werner called these episodes "Mystery Plays". They are the key points when a new awareness or threshold is reached by mankind. Werner listed maybe five of these Mystery Plays on the board and we broke into groups to act them out. We were each to select the group we'd like to join.

I noticed Werner was carefully observing which groups students were drawn to, and which characters they played. Some of these plays were Gilgamesh (the ancient Babylonian story of Noah), The Egyptian story of Isis and Osiris, there was an ancient Greek one, and King Arthur was the British Isles drama. I joined the Egyptian group, and I played Isis.

Anyway! Returning to this class on the episode of King Arthur; throughout the Dark Ages and at the time of King Arthur humanity had become cold and unfeeling. The general awareness was removed from qualities of Love and Understanding. Awakening the aspect of Love was a major task for the Hierarchy back then. Interestingly, Rudolf Steiner had pointed out it's often the same souls who "play a part" in these major awakenings throughout history. This is why many of us seem so familiar to each other and why we are involved in the same circles or endeavors.

These same souls are the ones involved in the major awakening episodes throughout history when new ways of thinking are introduced. In other words, many of us who are interested in New Age topics incarnate in groups. We come at the forefront of new impulses when significant thresholds are crossed. We form the backdrop of characters involved in those segments of history.

To some people the idea of reincarnation and other lives may still be hard to understand or accept. Jesus himself affirmed that each soul is reborn to live again. This is a necessary learning process which allows souls to grow in understanding and awareness. Jesus' acknowledgement of reincarnation is written in the Bible. The apostles told Jesus that people were talking of him being Elijah (some Bibles use the name Elias). Reincarnation was commonly understood at that time. Then they asked if this was true, if Jesus *was* Elijah in another life.

His response was no. *John the Baptist had been Elijah.* Jesus affirmed the reality of reincarnation in that statement. His parables of the continuity of life and the constant rebirth of plants and other living things also affirm this.

We discussed this topic at the Institute, and it was explained that originally the Bible contained many more references to reincarnation. All other passages directly mentioning it had been removed, except the one about Elijah and John the Baptist. They were removed both at the time of Constantine in the Fourth

Century and Justinius a few centuries later. Those in charge felt the concept of reincarnation was too difficult to understand. It was also a control issue among them. Rulers felt the knowledge that anyone could have been more significant than them would reduce their sense of importance. They feared it could produce anarchy.

It is believed that many, if not all, of the books and passages taken out of the Bible have been kept in a private library at the Vatican. It's also believed that all this hidden knowledge will someday be commonly understood.

Anyway, back to the class on Middle Ages. Werner explained how those who played a part in Jesus' life and crucifixion were the same souls involved at the time of King Arthur.

"The King Arthur episode", Werner said one day, "was another time when the aspect of Love was demonstrated and brought out. The same "cast of characters" who were around Jesus also played a part in the drama of King Arthur."

Again, it was such a provocative statement. We sat there for a few moments lost in thought, just imagining all of this. And then Werner continued.

"The twelve Apostles became the Knights of the Round Table."

I sat there on fire with curiosity. "Was Jesus Arthur?" I asked. The question was burning inside of me.

"No", came Werner's slow response. And he took another pause that seemed to go on forever.

"Jesus", he said at last, gazing into my eyes for an endless few moments, "... was Merlin."

How fascinating! Of course! He was the wise guide of Arthur who had a rare knowledge of life beyond what anyone else knew. Magic is, after all, anything that goes beyond the technology and understanding of the times.

"Merlin acted as the guide and teacher of Arthur", Werner explained. "This is often the case with great Masters. They're known as 'magicians' at the time because their actions defy normal laws of nature and the current level of understanding.

8a Merlin's Cave below Tintagel Castle.

In fact, in his time Jesus was known as one who could perform great acts of 'magic'. Later a different 'm' word was used for these actions however. They became known as miracles, but it's basically the same concept."

"Merlin was a key player in the King Arthur drama. He brought an awakening into the Dark Ages where people had grown cruel and without feeling. Once more he came to inspire and awaken mankind. He guided Arthur who was then able to demonstrate those qualities of love and understanding. The King Arthur drama became a step along the way in mankind's awakening process. It also helped pave the way for the much later Renaissance."

This was a phenomenal class and concept! I'm not sure anymore who he said Arthur had been, though I think he said Arthur was John the Baptist. And once again the "same cast of characters" who had been around at the time of Jesus played a part in another episode in history. Both times were major episodes when a great impulse for love was brought into a world that had grown cold and removed from much of a sense of caring.

The souls of Jesus, Mary and John the Baptist, he explained, had worked together closely in several lifetimes. Werner pointed out something I found very interesting. The two *episodes* of the Renaissance and the time of Jesus also have a strong connection. Many of the same souls were central figures in both "dramas". Rudolf Steiner had *seen* that many of the Renaissance artists were once very close to Jesus. This is why the Holy Family was often a subject for their paintings. Leonardo's memory was more conscious and his paintings are filled with codes and clues of who he had been. In the Madonna of the Rocks painting, Werner explained, the archangel Uriel pointing to John the Baptist was a clue that Leonardo had been John the Baptist. Also the child with Mary is John the Baptist, indicated by his rod. And the unusual folds on her lap are a hidden clue that the three of them also had lives together in the Himalayans.

8b Madonna of the Rocks by Leonardo

The same "cast of characters", as Werner put it, who played a part 2,000 years ago around Jesus would reappear again and again at key moments throughout history. Another interesting fact tying in with all of this was the lineage of Mary's family. They had Celtic roots. Mary and Jesus were both fair skinned, with finer and lighter colored hair than other people around them in the Mid-East. Mary carried that Celtic stream of energy into this crucial episode of the birth of Jesus.

Mary and Jesus were not only different in their more progressive ways of thought, but also in their physical appearance. Werner stressed that the reason Jesus and Mary were painted with fair skin and auburn hair by Renaissance artists was because those artists retained the soul memory. They had known both Jesus and Mary well, and painted them from a soul memory level. Joseph of Arimathea, who was Mary's brother, kept those British Isle connections. He was a merchant who traded among countries from the British Isles to the Mediterranean, and he sometimes took Jesus with him. Legends of Jesus visiting the British Isles can still be found throughout Britain.

It's fascinating how elements of previous lives often play a part in succeeding ones. Werner said that often the places we travel, especially to foreign countries, are places where we had been before in previous lives. This is why circumstances come about that bring us again to visit those places in our present lives. It is also why we often have déjà-vu experiences when we travel.

9

More Revelations and Instructions to Prepare for the Future

Fascinating information continued throughout those two years at the Waldorf Teacher Training Institute. We studied the lives of significant people in history from the aspect of spiritual science. We looked at what they had done in one life and how those acts and decisions affected the circumstances and opportunities of other lives.

We also studied the course of ancient history in the light of spiritual science. Our studies began in the far reaches of pre-history (by today's standards). We learned what people and souls were like in each Age, as well as details like what part of the world they came into. In a science-related course we studied the life forms on other planes or dimensions.

On the etheric plane there are life forms called elemental beings. There is a life or elemental being behind everything natural on Earth, including rocks, plant life and earth itself. Plastics and unnatural things have a way of subconsciously de-sensitizing people. This is why the Waldorf schools use all natural items wherever possible. On a subconscious level this facilitates the development of cognition and perceptiveness in the children as they grow and develop.

We also learned there are a few places on Earth where the etheric energy is particularly strong. In these places, Werner explained, the elemental beings sometimes become visible to people. He named three places where this energy is especially strong. Interestingly, they're all places near the water where there are rainy periods and the element of water mixes with the air and earth.

The British Isles are one of these locations, where the elementals are known as Leprechauns. Hawaii is another, where the elementals are called Menehunes. The Menehunes often play tricks on people. They live near the Pali Mountains on Oahu, where it rains often. My former roommate in Hawaii heard their little chattering voices in her house when she was pregnant and lived in the Pali area. I think the third location was Bali.

In our studies of the elemental beings, we also learned how different foods affect us. Werner explained that the elementals of some foods are not beneficial to humans, and therefore if one is very strict those foods are best limited or not eaten. This recommendation is for those wanting to avoid substances that could hinder expanding one's awareness. It was intriguing that Werner knew if we had eaten any of these foods when we returned from lunch. He could see it in our auras. I'm just passing this along, to give you a perspective of these foods as they exist on a finer level. Avoiding them all is next to impossible. For anyone interested, eating them in moderation might be a more reasonable plan.

Any of the foods from the "Deadly Nightshade" family, according to the Anthroposophists, are to be avoided for this reason. Interestingly, Werner spoke about foods that grow in darkness as ones to be avoided. Those include the "Nightshade" family, mushrooms and plants that grow underground, like potatoes and other tubers. Carrots are fine, because they get the sun's energy through their bushy leaves.

The "Nightshade" family includes: "Potatoes, tomatoes, sweet and hot peppers, eggplant, tomatillos, tamarios, pepinos, pimentos, paprika, cayenne, and Tabasco sauce are classified as nightshade foods. A particular group of substances in these foods, called alkaloids, can impact nerve-muscle function and digestive function in animals and humans, and may also be able to compromise joint function." From whfoods.com.

Another category of food Werner said to avoid is the legume family. If, that is, one wishes to limit anything that might hinder personal growth and awakening. This includes Acacia, Alfalfa, Carob, Chick Pea, Field Pea, Green Bean, Kidney Bean, Lentil, Licorice, Lima Bean, Mung Bean, Navy Bean, Peanuts, Peanut Oil, Pinto Beans, Soybeans; Soybean oil/flour/lecithin, Split Pea, String Bean. This was a great disappointment for all of us to hear! But it was also stressed that it's not good to be a fanatic about it either. Moderation is best, although I *will* say he was more emphatic about avoiding peanuts altogether.

I found it very interesting, as the energies are becoming more elevated on this planet and among society, food allergies are growing more prevalent. It has been especially evident with peanuts. Werner also discussed Pythagoras in this connection. He lived at a time when people were naturally more intuitive. Interestingly, Pythagoras forbade his students to eat legumes. He obviously sensed their effects, and he also wanted his students to be at their heightened potentials for both learning and growing in awareness.

One of my favorite classes was one on biographies. Studying biographies of famous people was a hobby for Werner. He could see their previous and successive lives, and he would trace how certain actions and decisions in one life led to certain conditions in a succeeding one.

One of the people we studied was George Washington Carver (1861-1943). Carver was born into a black family of slaves and yet he enriched humanity with many great accomplishments in his life. These included countless inventions all geared toward improving people's lives and helping society. He even worked with Thomas Edison and Henry Ford. One of the many items he invented was peanut butter along with dozens of other uses for peanuts. Carver understood there would be a demand for a crop such as peanuts. He wanted to provide farmers with a lucrative source of income. Because of the topic of peanuts, Werner's classes came to mind. In addition to agriculture, Carver was also gifted in the arts, sciences and horticulture. He was a significant soul, and very interesting to study; yet Werner was sure to recommend that we avoid peanuts.

Alcohol and substances containing alcohol were also cautioned against -- even rubbing alcohol that enters the body through the skin. Products that alter awareness go against human nature. They hinder and often prevent elevating energies and awareness. The very strict Anthroposophists even avoid nutmeg. It has a slight mind-altering effect.

As I said, the emphasis of this book is to share a deeper understanding of what's going on at this point in time on deeper levels of existence. It also includes some information about what will be happening in the near future. Werner would never go into much depth on any details of what *exactly* will be happening except to indicate it may look to some like a "cataclysm". In reality though, it will be a necessary shift and the outcome will be peaceful and in fact extremely positive and uplifting. This is why I felt that this information is so important to share at this point in time. When we understand what is coming, we will be able to recognize these Transition events as just the temporary path to a very uplifting and positive experience. I wanted to give people this understanding, however small it may be, of what we're heading toward.

What Werner stressed most strongly was to remain happy and calm. It is a necessary event and in the end existence will be tremendously better. He said to be close with family and friends and to spend time singing. This would certainly create a festive atmosphere of an adventure.

Much speculation and fearful scenarios have been told regarding what may be coming in 2012, so I wanted to give this broader and deeper view. What we *do* know is that the Mayans said *time will no longer continue in the same way* as of December 21st of 2012. They *never* said that time would *end!* If studied carefully that Mayan statement could indicate some kind of shift in the dimension of time. It is very interesting that scientists tell us there will be a major alignment of planets on this very same day: December 21st of 2012. They say it is a rare alignment that only happens roughly every 26,000 years, with a slightly lesser one happening at the midpoint, at roughly 13,000.

I find it so interesting that this scientific data goes along with the ancient Hindu and Tibetan spiritual view of the cycle of ages. Scientists on the Discovery and National Geographic channel programs say they expect this alignment to have some kind of effects on Earth. They just have no idea what those effects may be. I'm not saying this Transition will definitely be happening on that date. No one knows the exact date. Drunvalo, in fact, speaks of 2016. I'm passing along as much as I know so you can be informed in any case. Please understand that I'm not saying it will definitely happen in December of 2012.

This is something I want to emphasize though. Please remember, the *akashic records* also referred to as *the matrix* or simply the "record" of the future, is always in a state of change especially since the mid twentieth century. Werner said this unusual decision of so many Masters to live among us at this time has changed the *matrix* of the present and future. By this I mean that any predictions made are no longer totally accurate in timing. They could even be less accurate in content also.

Predictions are done by accessing what is known as the akashic records. This is the history of humanity as it exists on a spiritual plane. Details from the distant past, the present and into the future are all contained in the akashic records. Prophets and clairvoyants are usually accessing this when they predict things and see future events. Often they don't even realize they are reading the akashic records. The connection is often done subconsciously. Because of the unprecedented presence and activity of so many Masters at the current time as I just mentioned, reading these akashic records is no longer as accurate. Their activities and guidance is changing the future or akashic records. The presence of these Masters is affecting our present as well as our future so no predictions are totally accurate anymore. All we can do is to be as informed as possible for what may possibly occur.

In all likelihood we may never even see the cataclysmic events. Please remember, there is nothing to be afraid of, and I don't at all intend to worry people. I only want to pass along all the information I've learned from several very credible sources. It goes a little beyond other information given so far about this coming Transition. No one knows exact details of what will happen, but understanding as much as we can is helpful.

I have to caution that the "matrix" of events may have been altered again by now from what Werner had seen to be coming. This is the advice he had given in the mid-seventies. This scenario may not even take place now, but I wanted to pass along what he had told us.

He said there will be increased earthquakes, floods and other natural disasters. Eventually, right at the beginning of the Transition, he told us that there will be three days of darkness. Electricity won't be operating then either. He indicated that it is *very* important at this time to *remain both calm and happy.* We must think of it as an adventure that we are going through together. See it as exciting rather than as a frightful experience.

It will be very important, he said, *to stay inside* with friends and/or family and to know that everything will be all right in the end. It will be much improved in fact. Again, it will be important not to allow fear to take hold of you. When a sense of calmness is kept, even amidst what may seem outwardly like chaos, one's energy is kept at a high level and this way things will go more smoothly for us.

Just remember this if circumstances appear to be chaotic and the night lasts longer than normal. Know this is just something transitory and on the other side of those three days of darkness will be a wonderful life to begin again together. If this event should occur, the following instructions are important. These are the only practical instructions for preparedness I have heard, so I want to pass this along.

Werner said that, *if in fact those three days of darkness occur,* it will be important to close curtains tightly at the beginning of that period and to keep them closed throughout. Some have even suggested using duct tape around the edges of windows and outside doors. He wouldn't explain why this is advised, but it's been suggested that if there is a shift of the poles the resulting magnetic activity would be best not seen. There again please keep in mind that the future is now more than ever before in a constant state of change, so this Transition may well happen before any days of darkness even occur. My sense of his advice is that if views to the outside are blocked from us it will be easier to stay happy and cozy inside with friends and family. He said this big change is a time to stay positive. It is just the beginning, after all, of an incredibly uplifting and happy way of existence.

We asked if there will be a signal for when this is all beginning so we'd know when to prepare and close off all outside openings etc. The response was that there will be earthquakes across the southern Eurasian continent. (I've watched these carefully as they've happened over the years.) Then what will serve as the final signal is when Mount Vesuvius has a major eruption. It is then, we were told, that we should gather inside to our quiet, happy times together for those three days. I write this with a little reservation. While I wanted to pass this along so that we can be informed for any scenario, I also want to keep it open as the future is no longer "set in stone". We may not even see those three days of darkness.

What I've learned about this Transition is that it will be a dimensional shift this time. THis is the remarkable way it will be very different from the other Transitions that have occurred at intervals throughout the past. This dimensional shift will reportedly mean moving to a finer, higher frequency plane (dimension) of existence and could also include a shift through the dimension of time, as indicated by the Mayans. This may sound like science-fiction, but the existence of other dimensions is now recognized by scientists. What I want most strongly to pass along is the importance of staying positive, calm and happy as we ride out one great adventure into a happier existence and future -- however this is going to transpire.

Werner said to have candles and matches for light since there will be no electricity. It would be good to have sturdy hurricane type coverings for a candle or lantern that won't blow over I suppose. Battery-operated lights could be used. From a Waldorf or Anthroposophical perspective though, flames actually exist in the same form in other dimensions. They are very spiritual and both elevate energy and attract elevated energies. Flames are literally beacons on finer spiritual planes or dimensions. They attract higher energy and higher energetic beings to a place.

Werner most strongly emphasized *spending the time singing.* Telling stories and playing games with family and friends are other ways of keeping this a happy occasion, remembering that the end result will be better for everyone.

Those who are basically good people (and this translates into having a good energy level) will make it through this Transition successfully. To be reading this book is a good indication of being open to a deeper level of understanding. And this shows that your awareness and energy is positive.

Again, I know this may sound unbelievable or unlikely on one level. All I ask is that you're open just in case this information would come in handy. All we can do is to be prepared for any possibility, keeping this as "what if" information.

It's interesting that Eckhart Tolle's book *The New Earth* is geared toward overcoming hang-ups and psychological problems. He has used the term "pain body" to describe the part of us that holds onto negative experiences. This *hanging on* keeps us at a lower energy level and prevents us from moving on. It has been a major flaw in the human being and has stood in the way of more rapid growth and a higher level of energy. It's been a hindrance both to personal as well as national and global evolution.

In the end the "pain body" or the part of us that holds onto pains, traumas and negative experiences, has slowed the progress of life on the whole planet. Jesus and many other great teachers have taught people to move on without getting caught in the cycle of anger, vengeance or hurt. This has been a major hindrance to raising one's awareness and energy level.

Jesus said "turn the other cheek". His message was to just walk away without letting yourself get sucked into the lower energies. What matters more is maintaining an elevated state of presence and awareness. Involvement in negativity and maintaining a constant awareness of past traumas prevents growth in awareness and blocks positive experiences from entering one's life.

The whole human experience is one of passing tests and trials in order to grow and move beyond them. The legendary stories of higher beings battling negative forces that have attained access to Earth have been based on fact. To understand this it is necessary to understand the many dimensions to life. Call them "planes", or what Jesus referred as the "many mansions", or whatever you'd like. It all amounts to this; there is different life co-existing on many different dimensions at the same time. We live in a multi-dimensional universe. As we move into the future, more and more ideas that once seemed like science fiction are being understood as factual reality. Dimensions will be better understood as time goes on.

The fact is that there are many layers or levels of existence to everything we see. When I look up at night and see the stars and planets I wonder what they are like on other dimensions. I remember what had been said at the Waldorf Institute, that there is abundant life on every planet in our solar system. This life just exists on other dimensions. When I hear of astronomers stating that they haven't found physical proof of life out there, it strikes me as such a one-sided view. In a way it seems like such a "primitive" view, comparable to the ants who may be oblivious to the existence of human beings, cities and technology. It all exists beyond their level of sight. It seems more correct to state that *we haven't found* life rather than that there *is no* life in the places we have looked so far. As I see it our search has been far too narrow in scope. Or more correctly stated, searching for life in the universe only on this physical dimension is far too limited. It's been said that this physical dimension is one of the lowest dimensions.

I believe that there is much more life out there in the universe than we can imagine. That many other dimensions of life exist. And it could possibly be that this Transition, as a few clairvoyant people have indicated to me, will involve passing into another dimension, as futuristic as this may sound at first.

Here is an overview of the future scenario for Earth. This is another interesting aspect pointed out by credible sources. They are further details of this Transition I'd like to describe for you. When the Transition takes place and a large number of us become a part of the *New Earth*, here is the other side of that coin. This is an intriguing part of the whole scenario.

As I understand it, there will be a "split" in realities. A smaller segment of the population will take a divergent path. I'm talking about those who still harbor a lot of negativities and hostilities. Those whose energy has not risen to the level where they will be able to transition to this finer level of the *New Earth* will continue

94

their evolutionary cycle in the physical dimension. They still have refining to do and issues to work on in order to raise energies and awareness. The needed opportunities to continue their growth will be given to them for as long as they need it in order to refine their energy on the physical dimension. When they have reached a higher energetic level, they will move on from there. So this *New Earth* will co-exist with the *Old Earth*. The two realities will exist concurrent with each other, but on different planes or dimensions.

Understanding this is important. It explains why some clairvoyant "views" of the future may report a scenario with many struggles and strife. Some have also seen a relatively barren Earth with a much more scarce population. What they are seeing and reporting on is the *Old Earth* -- this planet and dimension that we're all familiar with. This may still continue on, but with a much smaller population consisting only of the ones who have more learning to do in this dimension for a while longer.

Since the *New Earth* scenario exists outside of the matrix or akashic records, views of the future are tuning into this dimension only. So prophets, remote viewers, hypnosis subjects and clairvoyants are accessing the physical dimension only. The new dimension, aka the *New Earth*, is beyond the matrix of what can be seen. These views and predictions are tuning in to the future of *this* Earth in this dimension and time frame only. It is the foreseen scenario of the *Old Earth*. This split in realities has made it difficult to get an accurate view of the total picture of what will actually be happening with this Transition. Understanding this dual reality split sheds a different light on the bleak views some have foreseen of the future. What is being reported is only the future they can see. It is *not the only future scenario* and it is *not the one* we will be transitioning to. What lies on the other side of this Transition is a very uplifted and positive existence for most of humanity. And the Hierarchy and Masters have been working hard to ensure that the largest amount of the population as possible will be making this positive Transition. We won't know any more details about the *New Earth* until we get there.

   I felt it important to give as much of an understanding as I could of both this point in time and what will be coming. This may sound so futuristic that it sounds fictional, but for example many of the scenarios and technologies in the earlier Star Trek shows have become reality.   The future is quickly coming upon us, and this knowledge could be helpful in the near future, whether it be at the end of 2012 or beyond that.

10

A Little Spiritual Cosmology

On a much finer plane or dimension there are higher beings
who sort of oversee life on Earth. The Theosophists and the
Anthroposophists acknowledge this and have broadened the
understanding of life on other planes of existence. They have
seen this to be, in fact, very true.

As I said in the previous chapter, the Anthroposophical view is
that there is life on every planet in our solar system existing on
other dimensions. Each planet and also many moons are lush
and green in another dimension. They all serve a purpose as a
place for life of some sort.

Werner had also explained that our moon, on another
dimension or plane, is the stopping off place where our souls meet
with our guides one last time before entering into the womb and
incarnating at birth. We make this stop on a finer dimension of the
Moon to discuss our plans for what we intend to accomplish and

work on in this lifetime on Earth. It is the location, in another dimension, for reviewing our life's intended goals one last time. In other words, it is the site for our final "briefing", and in that dimension the Moon is lush and green.

Those who succeed in completing most of their list of life goals are often the ones who go down in history as great examples and significant human beings. This is how relatively rare it is for one's intended goal list to be mostly completed.

Unfortunately it is relatively rare for anyone to complete the list of intended goals in their lifetime. The human experience is like an obstacle course that pushes us off track. Once we incarnate on Earth, despite all our best intentions, we are often overwhelmed by circumstances that hurt us or inflame our "pain body", as Eckhart Tolle would say. These elements divert us from completing or achieving all of our goals.

Earth in this physical dimension is, in many ways, a *danger zone*. The circumstances we need to deal with in our environment and within the family, along with the negative forces simply existing in this physical dimension can quickly overwhelm us. Souls or *human beings* are, in the end, very fragile and sensitive. It doesn't take much to 'bruise' or overwhelm us. Often we are overcome or worn down by ordeals. They actually change us from the more aware and purer beings we were born to be.

Werner told me one day looking deeply into my eyes, "The brighter the *light*, the more dark forces are attracted to it -- like flies to a flame". This quote has stayed with me. It gives a broader understanding of difficulties and struggles that may have come our way in life. Thinking of this I don't feel quite as bad about the rough times where it seems I've gone so far "backwards" or digressed in awareness.

So it is very true that when you meet someone such as a beggar or a criminal, you never know who they *really are* on a finer level. They may be a more advanced being that had become overwhelmed and changed due to harsh circumstances they experienced in their lifetime. As Werner said, very often the brighter the *light* of a person, the more negative circumstances and difficulties are attracted into their life. These forces try to render people ineffective and thus unable to complete their goals.

The negativities are extremely rampant in this dimension on Earth. There really are dark forces that try their hardest to create obstacles in one's life. They will do whatever is needed to disable one's personal effectiveness in life and in completing one's goals. This includes disturbing emotional challenges or the temptation to do drugs and on and on.

It is unfortunate how the allure to do drugs in the '60s and '70s was made even more enticing by people like Timothy Leary who asserted that it "opened your mind" and expanded your awareness. In reality it shuts down your innate sensitivities and abilities. Timothy Leary himself succumbed to the effects of lowered energy and awareness.

As meaningless as this may sound because it's been so overused, there is a great battle taking place at this point in time. It is a battle between the stubborn lower energy that won't move on to an enlightened existence, and the more elevated and aware element. The former will choose to stay with the *Old Earth*. Others will gladly move on to experience a more elevated way of being.

We've all chosen to be here now to be a part of this, although we may not consciously remember the choice. It just requires a great deal of discernment and resistance to what is not ultimately of a higher energy. The forces of Light are working in many ways to *awaken* as many people as they can to what is real and good. Expanding awareness in general has been a major goal of the forces of Light, and we can see this especially in all the movements that have happened over the past two centuries.

Another intriguing revelation explained in the class was the location where we as souls meet up again with our guides when we die or "excarnate", as Werner called it. When we die, he explained, our souls go to another dimension of Venus! He had explained to us that in a different dimension Venus is lush and green. This is the stopping off point where we discuss our lives with our guides and go over what we had accomplished in the life we just left. It's like our "de-briefing" location.

This is where I had gone during my near-death experience. Years later when Werner explained this it was a revelation and a confirmation.

I can totally understand how this may sound too fictional and idealistic to even consider. Believe me, I'm a big skeptic myself, *especially* where "new age"-type ungrounded ideas are concerned. I'd be skeptical of this information too, if I hadn't come into close contact with all these sources. You can't argue with information that comes from such a penetrating level of clairvoyance. There is no guesswork, speculation or imagination involved. It's simply seeing *what is.*

Music was another topic with celestial significance. It was an important part of studies as it nurtures the soul. Even traditional educators have found that music greatly improves the development of the brain and thinking. We studied the deeper aspects of music. Werner spoke of the *Music of the Spheres.* He explained that it *can* be heard on a spiritual plane, and consists of the pentatonic notes. These are the whole notes without C or F. The scale is D, E, G, A, B. I found this fascinating. Songs that are sung in the Waldorf preschool and early grades are encouraged to be in the pentatonic scale. Little harps or lyres are introduced in preschool and kindergarten and the children in the grades play natural wooden flutes called recorders.

There was definitely a reason for these experiences and crossing paths with these particular people was also meant to be. I hope sharing this with you is helpful. In the end this may be the reason for it all to have happened. So my next thought is this -- just imagine the scenario I've described is true. Imagine that the times we are living in are the most pivotal times in the history of the planet. I hope the contents of this writing may be informative to you, if only that you're open to considering it as a possibility.

11

Other Beings

Playing a Part

"There are more things in heaven and earth, Horatio, than are dreamt of in your philosophy."

William Shakespeare, from *Hamlet*

To give an even broader perspective on this whole future event scenario I'd like to describe a few more details. Added to the surprise of the Hierarchy and Masters being involved in future events, I've come to realize there are other beings who will be involved as well. Quite a few different sources have affirmed this.

To best explain this and to describe how I arrived at this place of understanding will involve telling a little more about my life. There are definitely incidents in my life I'd love to forget. I'd love to relive some moments over and to do them totally differently. But if I look beyond all the dumb mistakes, life experiences have given me insights and clearer understanding. This is what I'd like to share.

Unusual experiences and "coincidences" have run steadily through my life. Maybe they were instigated by a near-death experience at age nine, or maybe they started earlier than that. I couldn't go through all of these experiences or this book would be too lengthy. I'll mention a few that could be helpful to others in giving a broader perspective and understanding.

I'm adding a little aside here -- a little preview of what comes later in this book. I'll briefly explain an effective way to open your own potentials. This is a very important method for expanding your own abilities and perceptions. It will also put you in a position of being able to help others.

In 1970 I had learned Transcendental Meditation. It's a mantra meditation. A mantra is a sound used to quiet the mind. I've found that the most effective way of using a mantra is to repeat it silently on the in-breaths when you notice a thought entering your mind. I'll give further indications and sources for more information in Chapter 17. Mantra meditation is one of the most effective ways to broaden your awareness and also to tap into more of your potentials.

The goal of meditation is to bring your mind to a state of NO thoughts. A door to the infinite is opened when we can maintain a state of emptiness and silence. This triggers energy levels to increase. It's not an easy thing to do -- and constant sound or even the energy waves from TVs, radios, microwaves etc. make it even more difficult. But when, through persistent practice in meditation, you're able to reach periods of absolute SILENCE it's as if you're a battery that "recharges" during the silence. And over time you also expand in knowledge and understanding. You also discover that abilities and perceptions are gradually getting sharper.

There's another very effective form of mantra meditation called Transmission Meditation. It gives an added method for focusing your thoughts on the "third eye", which is also known as the ajna center. This allows you to sort of act as a "transmitter" of energy coming to Earth. In this way it's a very service-oriented form of mantra meditation, with a focus on helping the planet and others. See chapter 16 for more details.

I'll return now to discussing another level of beings who are also involved in this Transition. Quite a few sources have come to the understanding that "space brothers" or "aliens" are taking part in this. I know this may sound strange, but let me explain. If you look into the accounts of reliable and respectable people who have had encounters, you see there have been many of them. And you realize that this is a valid issue. It is only "disinformation" tactics that have caused the issue to be pushed to the background and clouded for as long as it has been. If you seriously research the issue, substantial evidence points to the fact that Earth has been visited. There are many more beings in existence than just the human race of planet Earth. Many sources believe extraterrestrial races are working in conjunction with the Hierarchy to help mankind on this planet.

Skipping ahead to 1977, a series of events happened that greatly broadened my understanding of life and the existence of life outside of this planet. One incident in particular made me realize we are not alone in the universe. This is something I feel will play into this whole future scenario. My reason for laying out this information is because I feel it is a definite reality that you should understand. I've learned from several reliable sources that these other beings will also be playing a part in what is to come.

In the summer of 1977 I met up with a favorite classmate of mine from the Waldorf Institute. Marilyn and I met between trains in Boston. We talked about what we had been doing in the year since we had seen each other. Marilyn said she had visited a healing center in Alamogordo, New Mexico where their method of healing was called Aura Balancing. At first my skeptical nature kicked in, and it struck me as unlikely and a waste of money.

Over the coming months though thoughts of this "Aura Balancing" kept resurfacing in my mind. I began to wonder if it could possibly correct some lingering visual problems from the near-death experience. The thoughts kept nagging at me until I had to check it out for myself.

I found their number, called and ended up making an appointment for a series of three Aura Balancing sessions. It all fell into place so easily that it was obviously meant to be. In another stroke of amazing synchronicity, some friends happened to be driving out west at the exact time. Their route would take them right through Alamogordo! So it was all set. In November of 1977 I went out to New Mexico for an Aura Balancing.

The meditation I had learned seven years earlier sharpened my intuitive abilities. When I arrived in Alamogordo I immediately got some very strong impressions. I was 23 at the time, and had known nothing about that area at all. When we pulled into town I got strong impressions of UFOs having visited the area. I "saw" them coming down in the hills in the past and I also "saw" that the occupants of the UFOs peacefully communicated with people living there at the time. They could have been Native Americans, later white residents or both. The strong impression left me "on fire" with curiosity to see if any local people had additional information. However, this was 1977. There was still a strong "laugh factor" involved in the whole UFO-alien issue. People tended to laugh at or ridicule anyone who took the issue seriously. So I brought the subject up very carefully at the house where I was staying. I was staying with a couple I'll call Mark and Pam Marshall.

"Do you ever hear about UFOs out here?", I asked them one evening.

Both Pam and Mark's eyes lit up with interest. I could tell it wasn't a new subject to them, and it didn't sound ridiculous to them either. They seemed interested in my question.

"We know a man named Dan Fry who was stationed on the base nearby. He had encounters while he was on the base and wrote about them in two books."

I was relieved when they took the question seriously and delighted to hear they knew something about it!

"Really? Tell me about his encounters!" Back then, in the '70s, you didn't hear about actual incidents where people described their encounters, and I was fascinated, and couldn't wait to hear more.

"They communicated first telepathically for four years before Dan actually met an alien. Wasn't that how it was, Pam?" Mark asked.

"Yes. They convinced Dan their mission was to help humanity and then over time a friendship developed between them and particularly with an alien named Alan." (Dan and those who knew him pronounced the name Ah-LAHN', with the accent on the second syllable and both A's sounding like short o's as in "top").

"The aliens indicated to Dan that there was a catastrophe in our future. They wanted to help mankind get through this. In preparation they needed to understand life on Earth in all its intricate details so some of them could come to live as human beings. It was implied that they were needed to guide people in certain ways of thought etc. Dan would be their contact or liaison who would help to make this all possible. Alan was the first one to come down to live as a human being." *alien*

"Amazing!" was the first word out of my mouth. "Did Dan say what they looked like?!"

"When Alan actually came to live on Earth, he looked human."

"It took four years of first communicating with Dan and learning all about Earth and humans before Alan actually came to live on Earth as a human being. Over those four years they would communicate telepathically. They were getting to know as much as they could about Earth, about the different cultures on Earth, the customs of Americans as well as other races etc. They asked Dan to choose books for them from the base library. They requested books on as many different subjects as he could get. Dan would get the books, put them out on a remote platform, and they'd teleport them to their ship. They'd then copy the books and have them back on the platform the following day."

I was absolutely intrigued! "Do you have the books Dan wrote about the encounter?!" I could hardly get the Marshalls to bring those books out soon enough! And I "devoured" them, reading them both over the next two days. There were two books back then. The actual incident was explained in a book called *The White Sands Incident*. And there was another one they had called *To Men of Earth*. It was a thinner booklet from Alan, and I found this one very interesting as well. They are now compiled into the one book called *To Men of Earth*. *from aliens*

"Is Dan Fry still in Alamogordo?!" I wanted to meet him, and to discuss the encounters with him in person.

"No."

My disappointment immediately turned to an ecstatic smile as Pam continued.

"They're now living outside of Phoenix, in a little town called Tonapah."

From Alamogordo it just so happened I was going on to Phoenix a few days later to stay with a sister and look for a job. I was elated! That would be the first thing I'd do when I arrived in Phoenix. I'd call Dan Fry and ask if I could meet him!

Back then the radio stations had something called *ride lines.* Universities also had *ride boards.* My plan for getting to Phoenix was to hook up with a ride. Times were simpler, people were more trusting, and everyone wanted to travel and discover America. So I went up to the local University on a hill in Alamogordo, found their ride board, and found a ride to Phoenix. It turned out to be with a cute guy in a red Trans Am with a Firebird painted on the hood. I'll call him Pete.

This would turn out to be the ride of a lifetime ... not just because of the cute guy or the red Firebird Trans Am! What made this ride special was the most intriguing conversation we had. More "top secret" details unfolded about the UFO - alien issue. They were details I never could have imagined. It was a wonderfully serendipitous connection, and it added more details to my understanding of UFOs and alien encounters.

Pete came to pick me up in his red Firebird and we started across the desert toward Phoenix. The land and the whole expansive atmosphere out there kept bringing up images. I'd look at that desert spreading off forever in all directions with the vast sky above, and the reality of other-worldly visitors kept coming to mind so strongly. I could "feel" their presence vividly out there! It was almost as tangible to me as the sky itself, and I wondered if Pete had any knowledge of UFOs having been seen in New Mexico. Little did I know the wealth of information Pete would provide on the subject!

"I just finished reading some books by Dan Fry", I said. "He was stationed on the White Sands Missile Base, and wrote about his encounters with aliens while he was there. Have you ever heard of any alien encounters?"

Pete looked at me with a knowing smile. His answer came as a welcome surprise -- and this ride to Phoenix became both a fascinating and an informative one!

"Actually I have an uncle who had Top Secret clearance in the military. One Christmas when the families were all together, the guys were in the kitchen having some beers and talking.

Someone asked my uncle about what he'd done in the military. He convinced my uncle to tell us something really interesting. So he started telling us about an incident."

Pete looked over at me again and smiled. "He wasn't someone who made things up. I know that what he was telling us was true."

"He said that one night he and some other guys in the barracks were suddenly awakened in the middle of the night. They had no idea what was going on, but there was some kind of an urgent mission they had to do. They were hurried into the back of a van and driven around until they lost their sense of direction. Then they were brought out to a remote desert location where they were told there had been a crash. They were ordered to gather and catalog all the remnants quickly."

I sat there mesmerized by this account. And the best was still to come.

"It turned out they were parts from a crashed UFO. "There were bodies among the wreckage." Pete looked into my wide eyes as I sat there listening intently."

Amazing! I never expected to hear such an intriguing story! It was the perfect addition to a drive across the New Mexico desert. Remember this was back in 1977. The Roswell incident hadn't been made public yet and this was all totally new information.

"Where did they take everything? Did he say?"

"He said they brought it to the nearby base and then he heard later they were taken to Wright-Patterson Air Force Base in Ohio."

What a fascinating account! I've often wondered whatever happened to Pete. He dropped me off in Phoenix, and went on to California where he was living at the time.

When the Roswell crash stories came out in the '90s the story was all very familiar to me. I realized that Pete's uncle was one of the guys who collected the debris.

12

Meeting Dan Fry

It was a Thursday afternoon when Pete dropped me off at my sister's apartment in Tempe. I walked in, said hi, dropped my bags and immediately got on the phone to call Dan Fry.

"Is this Dan Fry?" I asked a little shyly.

"Yes it is!" The loud voice of a cheerful grandfather answered back.

I introduced myself and said, "I've just spent a few days with your friends the Marshalls in Alamogordo. They told me about you and lent me your books, which I've just finished. I'm in Tempe now, and I'd love to come up and talk with you about your encounters!" I'm sure my excitement came through loud and clear.

Like I said, times were different then. People were more trusting and honest. Having stayed with Dan's friends was the only "in" I needed, and his response was equally as enthusiastic.

"Sure! We've got plenty of room! Why don't you come up for the weekend?" Dan's friendly voice was so welcoming.

Early the very next morning I caught a bus to the little town of Tonopah, Arizona. I arrived in this tiny town in a little over an hour and stood outside a little bus station looking for Dan. After a short wait an old station wagon pulled up with two older men inside. There were many mysterious bundles in the back end. It wasn't until then, for one brief moment, I wondered if I had been too naive and trusting to get myself into this situation where I didn't know these people. I still remember this flash of a feeling as I place myself back at that moment in time.

My doubts soon evaporated as Dan's warm voice shouted, "Hello Kristen! Welcome to Tonopah!" He hopped out of the station wagon and disarmed me with his friendly smile.

"Let me take your bag." I walked to the back of the car with Dan as he made room for the bag and slid it inside. When he saw me looking curiously at those bundles he quickly explained, "We publish a magazine called *Understanding*. And these are subscriptions I've got to mail."

Dan introduced his friend and we talked casually on our drive back to his place where there was a surprise in store.

114

12a *Dan's Tonopah residence, Nov.1977. There were several buildings like this with a small pyramid in the center where I'd meditate while there.*

We pulled into the driveway and I sat there amazed! Dan was living in a community of circular buildings with roofs like UFOs! Dan saw the surprised look on my face as we pulled up. "The buildings were here when I bought the property," he explained. "And I thought it could actually work out well. If any of them wanted to visit, they'd be sort of camouflaged."

And this is how my friendship with Dan Fry began. I'd spend a few weekends with Dan and Florence while I lived in the Phoenix area, helping them address and bundle subscriptions to their magazine. As we put on labels and bundled up the magazines, Dan told me the intriguing incidents of what it was like to communicate with and then to meet someone who was from another planet.

12b Dan and Florence, Tonopah, Arizona, late 1970s. DanFry.com

I felt like I got the sweeter end of that deal! Hearing Dan's experiences was worth far more than any help I gave in putting address labels on magazines!

It's not as special hearing Dan's words out of context. I mean, some would be much funnier coming straight from him. Like when he told me how strange it was to teach Alan to drive. He couldn't help but laugh as he told the story. It was a laugh that was infectious and just tickled you all over.

"Imagine this!", he said laughing, "Every time we got to a stop sign, obstruction or red light Alan would try to reach for some kind of lever to levitate the car over the intersection!", and he laughed all over again just thinking about the incident.

It *would* be weird, come to think of it, trying to teach someone with much more advanced technology how to operate a machine that must have seemed so "primitive" to him!

Something else that comes to mind was when we talked about the books Dan would get for them from the base library. He said they wanted a wide selection of many different subjects, to learn as much as they could about Earth and human beings. The most interesting book to them was our Bible.

The aliens told Dan their ancestors were recorded throughout the *Bible.* Their ancestors would often act as emissaries of a higher source. The word angel, in fact, means "emissary", he explained. The "ancient aliens" were described in the *Bible* as angels, Alan had told Dan.

Alan also told Dan that the passage stating *in the last days two brothers will be sleeping. One will be taken, and one will not* refers to the time of the Transition. It was explained to Dan that a certain level of awareness and energy will be required to make this Transition. No matter how close people were to each other -- they could even be sleeping in the same bed -- if a person's energy level isn't at the right place, they will not make this transition. Apparently, in order to cross the dimensions to this finer and less physical existence, one's frequency or energy level needs to be elevated to a certain extent. Alan explained that they were coming to live on Earth as emissaries to help in the effort to raise people's awareness in preparation for the *Transition* time, and to help as much of the Earth's population as possible. He explained that this whole mission was a joint effort along with beings from other dimensions also, because the planet is coming to an extreme point of change.

Dan brought up another interesting point Alan had told him. He had been told they had some *huge* ships, "They're miles across and as big as some of our cities!" He was told that they were monitoring Earth and a time would come when their presence would be needed. Until then they were staying close, but beyond detection. Back then, in the '50s and '60s, Alan told Dan these huge ships were "hiding in the rings of Saturn". I found it interesting that within the first decade of the 21st century NASA indicated they had found "anomalies in the rings of Saturn" ...

Alan's first job that Dan was able to get for him was as a trader or buyer in the Mid-East. He wanted to be there to interject peaceful thoughts and influence key people to make good decisions. It's unclear to me if Dan actually met others after Alan or if the other aliens "learned the ropes" from Alan and then became Earth residents on their own. All I know is that years after helping Alan, probably sometime in the '60s, Dan had been told there were many thousands of them living as human beings on Earth by then.

This next point is bound to raise a lot of controversy. I'm just reporting what had been told to Dan and what he told me. I found this fascinating. Alan explained to Dan that it was their ancestors who led the tribes of Israel through the desert for forty years. They were led by what appeared as a "cloud" by day and a "ball of fire" by night.

"It was a small space craft," Dan said. "Space craft have been known to hide themselves in clouds in the daytime."

"What was the purpose of wandering for forty years in the desert?" I asked.

"It was important", Alan explained to me, "that one entire generation passed before they were allowed to settle again in a town. The people at that time held such negativity and vengeance. It was 'an eye for an eye and a tooth for a tooth' mentality. Alan said that if this intervention had not happened at that point in time, a larger disaster would have happened in the future; a disaster that would have devastated humanity and possibly the Earth. So the tribes were isolated, 'monitored' and guided while one entire generation passed. And then they were allowed to settle again in a town."

I'd think about this statement many times since then. I wondered about the disaster that had been averted there ... If just maybe we wouldn't even have been around to go through this point of Transition if the exodus had never occurred. From what I've learned, this Transition is a major point of destiny we have to go through both as a race and a planet. This point of view also makes me curious about the "manna" falling from the sky, and what exactly it may have been.

I lived in Arizona for nine months from November 1977 to August 1978. While I was there I'd stay with Dan and Florence Fry a few more weekends. Then in August 1978 I moved to Colorado where I taught preschool for nine months. Meanwhile, from Colorado, I kept in touch with the Quimby community in Alamogordo, New Mexico. They encouraged me to move back to Alamogordo after that year of teaching and to open up a Waldorf oriented in-home preschool for some of their children. So in June of 1979 I moved down to Alamogordo.

You can imagine my surprise to discover that in the nine months I had been in Colorado, Dan and Florence Fry had moved to Alamogordo! What a strange *coincidence*, I thought at the time. In looking back over the years it would seem events had been "orchestrated" to work out as they did. I found a house to rent and made plans to have a preschool. It was nice to be back around the Quimby Center group, and getting ready for my preschool kept me busy.

Back then the Quimby community would meet on Sundays in a home they used for workshops. We'd have very nice, casual and friendly Sunday services there. One Sunday Dan announced at a service that a friend of his was coming to town. He was a psychic surgeon. A psychic surgeon is someone who can see into the body, find elements that shouldn't be there, and remove or correct them without surgery. They are able to reach right into the body

120

and remove things, perhaps by altering the energy of atoms so the arm and hand lose their physicality. They can pass right through solid objects or in this case the body.

There have been programs done on some people in South America claiming to have this ability, but they were proven to be fakes. The genuine ability is believed to be valid, however, but very few people are able to do it.

Dan went on telling us about his friend. "His name is Adin," he said. "And he's very good at what he does."

"Imagine his surprise when he found as a young boy he could reach right through solid objects!" Florence interjected with a certain nervous tension and high pitch in her voice. "One day he reached right through a window without even breaking it!"

I couldn't help but notice her nervousness along with her sort of forced, tense smile. It was as if she was desperately trying to portray Adin as an "ordinary" person.

Dan said his friend was in need of money and he wanted to help him out. He invited Adin to come to Alamogordo for psychic surgery sessions that Dan would arrange for him. There would be three sessions given over three days and the cost would be $100. That was big money back in 1977, especially for a "kid" in her early twenties. But a strong intuitive sense was nagging at me. It was an unmistakable *knowing* that Dan's friend was *not* from Earth. So I signed up for the sessions out of a strong sense of

psychic

curiosity. I wanted to meet this guy and also to see what his healing sessions were like.

Thoughts of Adin kept running through my mind that night. For one thing, the name seemed unusual to me. I had never heard the name Adin before. And besides, Dan never gave a last name for him ... I laid in bed wondering about Adin, curious also what his last name would be -- if he *had* one. And I *had* to create more time to observe and study this guy. I'd invite them to dinner -- the three of them ... Dan, Florence and Adin. Perfect! I finally fell asleep excited with the plan to invite them for dinner. It would be a great opportunity to observe and get to know this Adin a little better. The next morning I went over to the Center, hoping to catch Florence. And, sure enough, she was there.

"Florence! I'd love to have you, Dan and Adin over for dinner while he's in town!" I said with a cheerful note of enthusiasm.

"Well," Florence seemed cautious and unsure. Her answer came slowly and with much thought. "I guess it may work out ... I'll check with Dan and I'll call you."

And then Florence added with a tone of supreme importance, "Adin only eats fresh vegetables!"

"Ok, that's fine!" I said. It struck me as a funny statement, in the emphatic way she stated it. But it didn't matter to me since I never bought canned vegetables anyway. But it was just a momentary thought. My mind was preoccupied with the idea of

122

having Adin to dinner. She was sounding pretty positive it would work out, and I was feeling triumphant -- like I had scored a victory! I could hardly wait to meet Adin. Of course, I'd have to get the final confirmation after Florence spoke with Dan, but I was sensing that this "was a go".

There was one more burning question I was wanting to ask Florence.

"By the way Florence, I was wondering ... what's Adin's last name?"

Florence turned back around with the startled look on her face of a deer caught in the headlights. This was the *clincher* for me! I've never seen someone stammering so nervously! My question had caught her totally off guard, and she didn't know how to answer.

"Oh! ... Well, um! ... He ... He ...", and then she almost shouted very quickly, "He just goes by Adin!" with a smug sort of grin on her face -- pleased she found an answer and happy to forget the whole issue. She quickly turned back around to do whatever she had been doing.

The answer seemed to be so obviously contrived. It seemed suspiciously clear to me that Adin didn't *have* a last name. With each day that went by I was growing more and more curious and eager to meet this "psychic surgeon" with no last name.

13

Surgeon

From Another World?

The day finally arrived for the first of three healing sessions with Adin. Twelve people had signed up for them. This was an interesting number I thought. Twelve is a powerful number of groups with a focus or purpose. Twelve plus a leader, making thirteen in all -- as in the twelve Apostles and Buddha's twelve "Lohans" or disciples. We were all seated in the house used for workshops while two men I didn't know had gone to pick up Adin from the airport. The plane had been late.

I tried to meditate while waiting, but my thoughts were elsewhere. I couldn't stop thinking about Adin and what he'd be like. My intuitive sense was that he wasn't from this planet. I sat there wondering if I'd know which one was him when they arrived.

At last the door opened and three men entered talking among themselves. One was shorter than the others and he had an unusually high forehead. The most striking feature about him though, as a first impression, was that he walked with the most unusual glide. I had never before seen anyone walk with such a smooth gliding motion. He also spoke with a strange kind of lisp.

The men came closer and introduced Adin and themselves. They walked into the living room and Adin stood in front of the sliding glass doors. The glaring New Mexico sun shone behind him, and I was startled by what I saw. It was the strangest enigma. I had never, before or since, seen anything like it!

Standing against the backdrop of the bright New Mexico sunlight, I could see a "dark void" around Adin! That's the most accurate way I can describe it. Instead of any kind of a gentle auric glow, there was a *vacant* area around him. It wasn't negative "darkness", but more like a vacuum or *void* space which was black in color. It reminded me of the black void of outer space.

This baffled me! And yet there was absolutely *no* negative or heavy feeling about him. I thought and wondered about this for years afterward. Finally I came to the conclusion that his energy was probably so different even a sensitive person couldn't see any more than this. There was certainly not a "darkness" or negativity about him. Then again, it could be this was how his type of energy looked -- like the black void of space. There *was* another possibility. He *could* have been blocking anyone from seeing any kind of energy around him. Putting up blocks around oneself has been done before.

Actually I don't even see auras. This was the first and only time I had ever seen an energy field around anyone. And it left a lifelong impression. It must have been evident to me because of its striking difference from other people's auras on this planet. And, who knows, maybe we can subconsciously see auras all the time, and this one became evident to me because of its striking difference.

Adin was brought to the bedroom he would use for the healings and people began going in one by one for their sessions. Each session lasted about ten minutes or so. At last it was my turn. I walked calmly to the back bedroom, though I was actually on fire with a combination of excitement and curiosity.

The bedroom was small and a massage table was placed in the center of the room. The room was lit only by the ambient light through the window. I was given a hospital-type white gown and instructed to put it on over my underwear. Adin went into the adjacent bathroom as I changed and got up onto the massage table.

What he did first was to massage my closed eyes. I hadn't mentioned this to anyone, but I had rationalized spending all that money on those psychic surgery sessions with the thought it might help with some visual problems lingering since my near-death experience as a child. The Aura Balancing hadn't helped much

126

with this. So I was thinking Adin had intuitively picked up on my unspoken purpose for being there.

He began the session by massaging my eyes very vigorously, and then his fingers went right INTO my eyes! I clearly felt them pass *into* my eyes and then move around in there. He worked on each eye separately. It was a strange and sort of painful sensation.

"Don't flinch, and it won't hurt!" Adin cautioned.

It's easier said than done though! It's an automatic reflex reaction to flinch when something is in your eyes. And though I tried, I couldn't stop it from happening. This went on for quite a while, and by the time he was done my eyes were sore and feeling traumatized.

Adin then went into the bathroom and returned with a hot damp washcloth, which he laid over my eyes. Looking back on it, this was the perfect "cover" for him! This kept me from seeing what he was doing. I was dying of curiosity, and wanted to lift the corner of the washcloth to see, but I never did. I wondered if somehow I had been "programmed" not to peek.

Later I found out this was how he began everyone's sessions. And then he'd cover everyone's eyes with a hot damp cloth, so no one saw him working. Looking back on it, I wonder what exactly he was doing and what the purpose was of this eye procedure ...

He also worked on other areas for quite a while. When he was all finished he went into the bathroom, dropped something into the toilet and flushed it. After washing his hands he came out to speak to me.

"I removed mucus from your pancreas, and corrected varicose veins that would have formed in the future."

This was an interesting statement. Thinking back on it now, it's nothing that can be proven. I never felt anything other than honesty and trustworthiness from him. There was a certain unspoken understanding between us. I was glad to have met Adin and felt somehow very familiar with him. I also felt willing to help him if I could.

When the session was over I stood and pulled on my white pants under the hospital gown. I didn't want to waste a minute where I could be talking with Adin, and there was absolutely no sense of having to be modest with him. I was very interested in his views and thoughts. He seemed to have depth of insight and perception on many different topics. As I stood there in that first session, face-to-face with Adin, I saw some very unusual things. They are images that still remain with me. I can't explain how, but I clearly saw that his real etheric hands were more like "claws". And I clearly "knew" and could "see" that his hands from the forearm down had been altered to look human. I could also see that his facial features had been altered to look human. His real (etheric) face did not look human at all.

During his entire stay in Alamogordo, Adin wore a long sleeved shirt with a crew neckline, and socks and shoes covering his feet (no sandals). The only skin visible was his hands, neck and face. I couldn't help but wonder what the rest of him looked like under the clothes.

We talked about many things including the Earth, the United States and humanity. I regret that I don't remember specifics about what was said over those three days of conversations with Adin. All the conversation was totally overshadowed by a gripping statement he made during the third session. It totally blew me away. What struck me most vividly the first day were a few statements he made. They clearly indicated to me that he realized I knew his true identity and it seemed to me he was fine with it. Later over dinner I found out he was still attempting to present himself as an ordinary human and citizen of Earth -- despite some mannerisms and statements that seemed to contradict what I observed.

The day of my first session with Adin was going to be a busy one for me. I had business things to do in preparation for my preschool. My bike was outside and from there I had planned to ride downtown to register for an in-home business at City Hall. The name I had chosen for the school was Palace Gate Preschool. I had designed promotional enrollment flyers and was delivering them to pediatric offices and to other locations. (I had drawn a Taj Mahal type palace on the cover with the name "Palace Gate Preschool" below.)

As we stood there talking Adin looked uneasy. It was like he was *seeing* my plans for a busy afternoon.

"I suggest you go home to rest for a few hours first". His voice sounded sort of urgent, as if it was almost mandatory.

"No, I'm fine!" I assured him. "I have lots of errands to do! My bike is outside, and I need to ride downtown to make arrangements for the preschool I'm starting."

I could see that he was distressed with my answer, but I felt fine and had much to accomplish that day. I never found out why resting after the session was so important to him, but I pieced things together over time. Throughout our conversation Adin would interject that I should go home to rest a few more times.

My healing sessions lasted much longer than anyone else's because of our conversations. For this reason I was called in last for the next two sessions. On the way downtown I stopped at a school having summer sessions. I needed to use the restroom. I was surprised to see a red dotted line diagonally across my lower belly. It lasted several days until it faded.

At my second healing session Adin used terms like "your people" and "your president". This made it seem obvious he was speaking to me as a confidant. His conversation sounded very much like advice from a knowledgeable analyst with a deep understanding of events in the country and the world. To me these conversations substantiated my first impressions. It seemed evident this was one of Dan's friends from *off-planet*. It also seemed clear to me that Adin was comfortable with my knowing his true identity. All indications were Adin realized I knew who he was, and he was fine with it.

It was at the third session Adin said something which had an upsetting impact on me. He stared intently into my eyes for a few moments and said, "*You know*, don't you?"...

It was a provocative statement and filled with such mystery! Know what? ... And yet on some level we were sort of *in sync*. We had an intuitive connection and level of understanding. He continued looking deeply into my eyes and again said, "*You know* ... You know that we are the *last* generation to fully grow on this planet as it is."

On some level I *did* know there would be massive changes in the future for both humanity and the planet. But still, as a 20-something with my future ahead of me, this statement really freaked me out. It brought such a sense of finality -- that life on this planet as we know it would be undergoing a total change. What I've come to realize, however, is that life is *not* going to be coming to an end.

Even if there *is* a period of chaos and cataclysm where it LOOKS like disaster and "the end", it's only a *Transition* taking place. It is a change the majority of the Earth's population will be making. It's all set up for us to make it through this Transition. It's frustrating trying to explain this. I'm a very skeptical person myself because I know it sounds like science fiction. But what I've come to realize is there will be a Transition or *shift* into a finer dimension. The *New Earth* and our bodies themselves will become less densely physical. We will be transferred to live onto a *New Earth*. It's really the most incredible adventure in the billions of years of history of this planet. And we'll take this ride together!

The reason I mention this whole issue of aliens or "space brothers" is because all indications point out they are one more entity or non-Earthly race that has also been observing and interacting with the Earth and humans. They have been monitoring our development. And, like the Hierarchy or Masters, they are also beings that have come unrecognized. They have come to live on Earth in order to help and be a part of this major event.

Some may think this is naive thinking -- this fairy tale-like scenario of great and kind beings coming to rescue us and make everything right. Believe me! I'm a skeptical and analytical person myself! I realize how this may sound. It's something that has become very evident to me though. My life has crossed paths with various people and situations which made this all very clear. It has all pointed toward this same scenario and I thought it would be less shocking to be a little familiar with these concepts by reading of them. So if and when this scenario begins to take place it won't be so new. You'll at least be somewhat informed about what's going on.

Why have these things come into my life? I'm not sure, but there seems to have been a reason.

132

14

Dinner with an Alien

?

The day arrived when Dan, Florence and Adin would be coming for dinner. Remembering Florence's cautionary instructions, I went to the market and got plenty of nice fresh vegetables. I came home, cleaned them, cut them up and made a large pot of vegetable soup. I also had rolls, salad and fruit for dessert.

My guests arrived and I showed them around the small house where I was preparing for the preschool children. Then we went into the dining room. Adin sat to my left. Dan was directly across from me and Florence sat opposite Adin.

I served everyone's dishes and as I set them on the table I made the remark, "I bought lots of nice fresh vegetables at the market and made this healthy vegetable soup."

As I set Adin's plate in front of him I suddenly got a very clear realization of what Florence had meant by "fresh vegetables". She meant RAW vegetables! I wished she had said that. And I was disappointed not to have what Adin would like. He ended up not eating much. He *did* have some salad though, and just a few spoonfuls of the soup.

Our conversation was pleasant, but it was evident Adin wanted to present himself strictly as a regular guy "from these parts". At one point, however, something very interesting happened.

Adin asked Dan, who was seated across the table, "Have you made any progress getting my green card?"

Dan responded that he was still working on it and started explaining exactly what was happening.

Meanwhile my thoughts were going ninety miles an hour! I was trying to figure out *where* Adin was from if he needed a green card! He spoke perfect *American* English. And I'd certainly recognize the accent if he were from any other English speaking country. I'd even recognize a Canadian accent. He had no accent at all! His way of speaking, both in the phrases he used and the way it sounded, was totally American! So where would he be from if he needed a green card?

At a brief pause in their conversation, I turned to Adin and interjected, "What other languages do you speak?" It was actually

134

a question that fit in with their conversation at the moment. This was my little way of determining his possible origin.

"None, just English", Adin said quickly. Then he turned back across the table and continued his conversation with Dan.

"Isn't that interesting?" I thought. And my thoughts returned to Adin's identity and the green card issue. It seemed like one more bit of evidence he was from *elsewhere*! My thoughts were totally occupied with this whole issue.

What happened next was bizarre! I can still *see* it, just as if it were yesterday. It's a permanent image in my memory. While speaking to Dan, it was like Adin suddenly *heard* my thoughts! All at once he stopped in the middle of a sentence, turned to me and stammered,

"My family traveled around a lot while I was growing up. We ... we lived on islands mostly ... and I just ... I had a block to picking up any other languages!"

He said it quickly, and with the tone of a desperate plea. It struck me at the time as such a blatant spur-of-the-moment excuse. It reminded me of Florence's quick explanation when I asked her about Adin's last name.

There was one other issue. Dan mentioned something about Chicago, and Adin's question struck me as kind of strange.

"What kind of a *town* is Chicago?"

He asked this as if he knew nothing at all about Chicago, as if it were a totally foreign or *alien* place to him. This struck me as strange because anyone who grew up on the planet knows about Chicago, and knows that it's a city and not a *town*. And anyone who speaks *only* American English would especially know a little about Chicago -- where it is and that it's a large metropolitan city.

One last thing that seemed a little unusual was Adin's behavior after dinner. I invited them into the living room and Adin seemed very uneasy with this. He obviously didn't know the purpose of us sitting in the other room. It was like it didn't seem "logical" to him. He seemed totally unfamiliar with social conversation which didn't have a definite purpose.

Adin left the next day and life returned to normal. I kept busy with my preschool preparations.

15

A Mysterious

Time Loss Incident

Three months later Mom came out for a visit. By then it was around November. Winter was approaching and it was getting dark earlier.

Mom rented a car and one weekend she, a friend and I drove up to Taos. It was a few hours north of Alamogordo. We stayed in an old hotel on the town square and had a fun weekend. Sunday evening after dinner we headed back to Alamogordo.

I let Naomi sit in front with Mom, and I sat alone in the back seat. We were driving back on a very dark fall night when suddenly, out of the blue, a milky whiteness surrounded everything! All at once the whole area looked like it was enveloped in a thick white foam -- in the middle of the New Mexico desert! It was the most dense fog I had *ever* seen, and all the cars pulled over. There was a definite creepy feeling to it all. The circumstances just seemed so bizarre and out of the ordinary -- almost like it had been "staged". Added to that, all the vehicles except for our car were RVs, and it felt a little like "the invasion of the RVs"!

Strangely, way out in a field *directly* to the left of our car was a *huge* glowing red ball. You could clearly see this perfectly round huge glowing ball through the dense fog.

I stared out the window to my left, intrigued with this strange object. "Look at *that*! What in the WORLD could it *be*?" I almost shouted as I sat there, captivated with this strange image.

Mom and Naomi were absorbed in casual conversation and not paying attention to anything else. Mom turned and quickly glanced out the window. In sort of a disinterested way she said, "Oh, it's probably a farmer having a bonfire".

"Mom!" I said, "Even in this dense fog, if it was a fire we'd be able to see the leaping flames. It wouldn't be a perfectly round ball!"

But the mind tends to make excuses for strange anomalies. Mom and Naomi's thoughts were on other things. I had a strong urge to walk out there to see exactly what that huge glowing ball was, but the fog was *so* incredibly dense! I wouldn't have been able to see any ditches or holes, so I decided against it.

Then something even stranger started happening. It was incredibly eerie! The antenna on the front right corner of the rented car started to rotate. It moved slowly in circles at first, like it was inscribing 8 inch rings in the sky. We all just stared at that antenna -- it was *so* bizarre! Then it picked up momentum, moving steadily faster and *faster*! As it sped up it flung farther and farther out until it was whirring around completely flat, 360 degrees, on the top of the hood. It looked like the whirring blades of a helicopter, creating the illusion of a large disk like helicopter blades do. It was the weirdest thing! And yet it didn't break.

For many years afterward Mom would tell her golfing buddies about that incident. It was so bizarre! Was something interfering with the magnetic field around our car?!

A little while later I leaned forward and asked, "Naomi, what time is it?" Because I leaned forward I actually saw the clock before she answered. It read 7:10.

"Ten after seven", Naomi said in the midst of their conversation.

In the *very next instant* I was again leaning forward and asking Naomi what time it was. But this time, literally in a flash, the fog, all the cars and the strange glowing red ball were all ***gone!*** In an instant we were sitting alone on a dark abandoned looking road. The antenna was suddenly standing still as a pole, and strangest of all was that the clock had suddenly *jumped* from 7:10 to 8:20 in an instant! The clock hands, against all logic, abruptly leapt ahead an hour and ten minutes. But there was no logic to anything that had just occurred.

"Twenty after eight", came Naomi's matter-of-fact answer, and they just continued with their everyday conversation! Totally oblivious to what had just happened.

To top it all in "high strangeness", they were still on the SAME SENTENCE! It appeared as if the contents of our car had been *frozen* for an hour and ten minutes. From the inside of our car life seemed to continue "seamlessly". We perceived no gap. Mom and Naomi went on with their conversation seemingly without a hitch. When their sentence began, however, the surroundings as well as the clock were totally different than when it ended a few seconds later!

"Oh look," Mom glanced out the window nonchalantly. "The fog is gone, and all the cars are gone. I guess we can go now!"

She cheerfully started the car as if nothing had happened, not seeming to notice all these sudden changes. I guess it was because they were totally preoccupied with their conversation.

We traveled back down the road -- alone on a pitch black night heading south. It must have been a new moon, because after that fog vanished it was totally pitch black darkness. The eerie ambiance lingered as we made our way down the deserted highway going south toward Alamogordo.

The whole incident was something I'll never forget. Decades later when I asked Mom about it, what she remembered was the spinning antenna.

I couldn't help but wonder if there was any kind of connection between this strange incident and Adin. Over the next week or so another incident developed that quickly answered this question in the affirmative. It is another story all in itself, which isn't really pertinent to this book.

Bottom line from this whole incident is it solidified the reality of other types of beings. It also broadened the understanding of this life as a multi-dimensional existence, just as scientists have acknowledged. And there are times, in this multi-dimensional existence, when the "rules of nature" as we know them don't hold true.

I'm telling this because I sense big changes in the future. It is my hope this book will help people adjust and move forward with these changes. Understanding brings confidence and allows the determination for positive action.

****

There's one last thing about Alamogordo I'd like to share. The white sand is incredible! It is now occupied as the White Sands Missile Range. During the daylight hours the public is allowed to visit and walk on the sand.

15a Mom on the White Sands, 1979.

Those sands emit a wonderful energy! Some of us from Quimby would go out there just to walk and lie down on the sand. I recently discovered the sand is finely ground selenite. No wonder it has such incredible energy!

Selenite creates protection around you. It's also known to connect you to higher frequencies, especially in meditation, as well as connecting you to your angels or guides.

In the following years I eventually moved back East. Dan moved to Virginia Beach. Florence passed away but Dan and I continued to stay in touch. We exchanged Christmas cards for years until one January in the eighties I got a letter threatening me never to send her husband a card again! I didn't realize that Dan had remarried, and it turned out she was a younger and very possessive person. I learned this from someone else who had known them. We stopped exchanging the cards, and that's when Dan and I lost contact with each other. I read that Dan eventually moved back to New Mexico. He died in Alamogordo in 1992 at age 84.

Bottom line is that aliens, or "space brothers" are real. What I've discovered is that their agenda is to assist mankind with the tremendous "shift" or Transition that is coming. They have been working in cooperation with other beings including the Hierarchy to ensure that the majority of humanity will make this Transition successfully.

16

"Coincidental" Meeting

and More Verification

Decades passed with experiences and "coincidences" continuing to run through my life. Then one morning, in June 2007 I woke up with an out-of-the-blue certainty that there were three books "waiting for me" at a certain used bookstore in a distant part of town. I had never been to that bookstore before. I knew that two of these books were about the Masters and one was by Ingo Swann. Ingo developed the military's system for training psychic spies called Remote Viewing. Many of his books are out of print and some of them sell for hundreds of dollars.

That afternoon a friend and I went out to this used bookstore. I walked in and asked where the spiritual and metaphysical book section was located.

"Go down to the third aisle, turn left and walk to all the way back. They'll be on the left at the end of the aisle."

So I went to the third aisle, turned left and for some reason I looked immediately at a shelf to my left. My eyes fell on the orange spine of a book titled *Extraordinary Times, Extraordinary Beings: Experiences of an American Diplomat with Maitreya and* *Book* *the Masters of Wisdom* by Wayne Peterson. That book had been out of place! And it was obviously one of the three books out there "waiting for me"! I continued on to the end of the aisle where my friend Karen was already looking through the metaphysical section. The next book to catch my eye was *Letters of the Masters of Wisdom* by the Theosophical Society.

There they were! Two of the books I had sensed were there for me! Whether or not I'd find a book by Ingo seemed doubtful though, since they are rare. But I continued looking diligently, just in case.

After a few more minutes of looking, *there it was!* *Everybody's Guide to Natural ESP: Unlocking the Extraordinary Power of Your Mind* by Ingo Swann!

I went home and started reading the first book I had found. Wayne Peterson's book called *Extraordinary Times, Extraordinary Beings*. Life intervened though. After reading over half of the book I got so busy, I didn't pick it up again for a couple months.

One day in late August or early September of 2007, I was dashing out the door to sit at an art show booth, and my eyes fell on Wayne's book as I was running out the door. So I brought it along to finish reading it once and for all.

As I sat there engrossed in reading, I was surprised to read toward the end of the book that Wayne had been guided to move out to Las Vegas of all places! A series of "coincidences" led him to finding a certain house he had had a vision of not long before. And it was in Las Vegas.

"That's funny", I thought. I was going to Las Vegas in October to the International Remote Viewing Conference. I had to book my flight, as a matter of fact, the very next day to still get the best airfare deal. So I whimsically thought to myself, "Hmm ... I'd love to meet Wayne Peterson! ... If I could meet him, I'd book my flight for a day early. I'd fly in on Thursday to meet and have dinner with Wayne Peterson!"

It was only a fantastic whimsical thought. Realistically, how could I possibly connect with an author overnight -- in time to book my flight the next day? I'd have to write a letter to the author in care of the publisher. Who knows when and if it would ever reach him! It was just a silly idea, and nothing that could be arranged overnight ... or so I thought!

I continued reading, until I came across another "coincidental" circumstance. Wayne wrote that after he had moved into the complex in Nevada he discovered Dannion Brinkley was living in the same complex. He also implied that he and Dannion would be working toward the same goal in the future of helping humanity and helping to carry out the work of the Masters.

Dannion Brinkley is a guy who had been struck by lightning twice. He had three near-death experiences that totally changed him around from a one-time bully to someone devoted to helping others. A total transformation had occurred, and he's now devoted his life to helping others, after having connected with beings on "the other side". He's especially involved in helping veterans. I had seen a few programs on Dannion and had also read a book or two by him about his experiences. Then "coincidences" led me to meeting Dannion on a flight in the middle of the night in December of 1999.

Thoughts were rushing through my head! This was another funny *coincidence*! It seemed like some sort of destined connection was going on here! I wondered, "Could these all just be *coincidences*?"

I had met Dannion when I was flying home from Egypt in December of 1999. It was the middle of the night, and the plane was over the Atlantic. The cabin lights were turned very low, and everyone around me was asleep. I was seated on the right aisle, maybe six or seven rows back when I see this man come back from first class over on the left aisle. He crosses over to the right aisle and heads back toward me. Because of the programs I had seen and the books I read, I recognized the man. It was Dannion Brinkley!

Coincidentally there *happened* to be an empty seat beside me. I moved over and Dannion sat down. He had gotten the message that there was a girl in coach class he needed to go back and meet -- and it was me. We talked and exchanged near-death experiences until people around us asked us to be quiet. They were trying to sleep.

I didn't think so much about this until we arrived at the New York Airport. While walking down a busy concourse I saw Dannion a short distance ahead of me. He was lost in animated conversation with a woman. I sensed she was his partner guide on an Egyptian tour and they were just returning to the United States. He was loudly and enthusiastically telling her about someone, when he turned around and saw me.

"Look! *There* she IS!" he shouted with equal enthusiasm.

It was then that I "grokked" the whole scenario. I intuitively got it. I sensed I would meet up with Dannion again, and we'd be working toward the same goal of helping the Masters at some point in the future.

There I was, reading Wayne's book, and captivated by these two "coincidences"! When I got home from the art show I threw the book on the coffee table and got the impulse to email someone in Canada. Years earlier this guy and I had exchanged emails about Maitreya. I got online and emailed this man.

"Hi Todd!" I wrote. "I just finished reading a book by Wayne Peterson called *Extraordinary Times, Extraordinary Beings.* He sounds like an interesting person. Have you heard of him?"

"Wayne wrote in the book that he had recently moved to Las Vegas. It just so happens I'm going to Las Vegas for a Conference in October, and I was thinking I'd love to meet him while I'm there."

I typed all this, just sort of wishfully "thinking out loud". They were just wishful thoughts that I never really dreamed would become reality.

Lo and behold! Todd just "happened" to be online at that very moment! And, most surprising of all, he knew Wayne Peterson personally! Todd forwarded my email to Wayne who emails me and invites me to dinner in Vegas!

Boom! Boom! Boom! It all came together like that! So the next morning I booked my flight for Las Vegas a day early. I flew in on a Thursday to have an extraordinary dinner with Wayne Peterson!

The Remote Viewing Conference that year was at an unusual hotel for Vegas where there were no slot machines. So there was none of the noise and commotion that would have been hard on me as an intuitive type sensitive person. The buildings were white and tan adobe with clay-type roofs, and the property extended back a long distance. The buildings surrounded a long courtyard with two pools. This serene enclosure was dotted with palm trees. It felt very much like an oasis in the midst of Las Vegas and it gave me the feeling of being in Egypt. My building was at the very back, and that long walk everyday reminded me so much of Egypt. It made my whole stay in Vegas feel like a rendezvous with faraway other times and friends.

Wayne picked me up that evening and whisked me off to the magnificent Bellagio Hotel -- which was very much an *other-worldly* experience in itself! He gave me a little tour of the over-the-top hotel and then we went to one of the restaurants for something to eat. It was one of the most fascinating evenings and conversations of my life! Wayne told me in person about his experiences of meeting the Masters written about in his book, and more. We talked for hours. Eventually we left the restaurant and ended up sitting on some chairs in a hallway to continue our conversation. Wayne told me in detail about his meetings with the Masters and their plan to help humanity. It was another incident that furthered this scenario I had learned so much about over the years. It was fascinating to hear of his meetings with these evolved beings from a finer dimension.

We also discussed how other beings on different levels are playing a part in this whole event. Most interesting to me was Wayne's account of what the Masters had told him. They explained that the Earth and most of its residents will be passing through a dimensional shift. This would be a necessary Transition. The bottom line is that it will work out all right. We're going to make it through this and things will work out well in the

150

end. In fact, life will be amazingly wonderful after we pass through this Transition.

It's important to understand this is a necessary Transition, and in the end things will be fine. If one realizes this when things start happening, it can help you move through it with a focus on the end result. Any type of fear or uncertainty can be transcended with understanding.

What was made clear all over again is that this future scenario has been well worked out. All the "players" are in their places. We *will* make it through this Transition. It could possibly occur before catastrophic changes even begin. This is a very significant time for both Earth and humanity. All sources I've crossed paths with agree that we have chosen to be here now to take part in this change. It is clearly a point of destiny in which the souls of humanity and Beings from other levels and dimensions have chosen to participate.

Again, I realize this may sound unbelievable and unrealistic. Definitions of "reality" are broadening however. As time moves forward what is written here will be more and more easily understood. I'm sharing this to give a future scenario with more of a basis in what _will_ be, rather than all the negative speculation out there -- especially where 2012 is concerned. The negative views of what might happen are just speculation.

The information I've written here comes from an accurate source of knowing, rather than merely negative speculation.

17

The Power of

Meditation

The purpose of meditation is to train the mind to reach its maximum state of effectiveness. This state is when the mind is totally quiet without being distracted by constant thoughts. It's amazing, but this is how the optimum mind state is reached. When the mind is silent, those quiet moments become "reactivation" periods -- literally. The everyday world we live in sabotages us daily from being able to function in full control of our capacities. When you're able to regularly silence the mind through meditation, your abilities as well as your mind itself function optimally.

A "mantra" is a word or phrase. Mantra meditation uses a high frequency word or phrase that you repeat silently to yourself to quiet the mind. It's a tool for training the mind to reach the state of silence. This is the goal of meditation. The silence allows your mind to "recharge", like a battery.

The best mantras I've found are either Aum (ah-oom') or the shorter version which is Om. They are sacred sounds which have a particularly high resonance and energy. It is best to sit in a quiet room. I light a candle, which creates even more of a sense of serenity. Sit either in a chair, or on a bed -- whatever is most comfortable. You can sit either cross-legged, feet on the floor or have your legs straight in front of you if you're on a bed. Some people even meditate lying down. I find that an erect spine helps with the focus. To me if you're lying down it's too easy to drift off into sleep.

Take three slow, deep breaths, then on the fourth in-breath silently say the mantra to yourself. It helps, for me at least, if you repeat the mantra to yourself on the in-breaths. Remember that the goal is to let your mind drift off into silence, with no mantra. The mantra is only used to focus the mind. With practice the goal is that the mantra silences your mind so you drift off into a state of perfect silence, without repeating the mantra. When you notice yourself thinking about something is when you bring your focus back and repeat the mantra silently again. This creates another chance for the mind to achieve silence.

Here's a very important aspect of meditation, especially when you're starting out. Thoughts will come in. All the things you've got to do, the lists you need to make etc. etc. will run through your mind. It's normal. The important point is to not get impatient or exasperated to the extent of wanting to give up. Thoughts are all right. Each thought is like a bubble of tensions being released, bringing you closer and closer with practice to a state of serenity. Thoughts are symptoms of the everyday tensions inside of you. So as each thought is released your mind gets more and more quiet over time. When you recognize that you're thinking about something simply take another breath and repeat the mantra. Don't let the thoughts discourage you from persisting with it, because they're a part of the process. With each thought released it gets easier.

Silence is your ultimate goal. And once you reach a state of no thoughts it really feels incredibly good. It's sort of a euphoric feeling, or a "natural high". Not that we're going after a "high", but this is what happens. It's called *samadhi*, which is an Indian word meaning superconsciousness.

Twenty minutes is a good starting amount of time. It's good to work yourself up to a least a half hour. Many people meditate for longer than this -- for an hour or more in some cases. It's also good if you set a time to do this regularly. Every morning or day sometime would be great. Or maybe a few times a week.

Transmission Meditation is a very powerful form of meditation that connects with the Masters. While silently repeating the mantra in Transmission Meditation the focus is kept on the third eye center. This is called the ajna (azh'-na) center, located between the eyebrows. The mantra "Om" is usually used.

In addition to keeping the attention at the ajna center or third eye, the important feature of Transmission Meditation is that it begins with speaking a prayer called the Great Invocation out loud. Speaking this invocation out loud actually draws Maitreya to you.

This is done either in groups or individually. There are many Transmission Meditation groups that meet regularly around the world. Sound is very significant. Just as tones in music are effective in creating and drawing certain energies, the purposeful sound of the voice is extremely effective here. Speaking the Great Invocation sets up a connection with the Masters of Wisdom, which then direct energies to you in just the frequencies that you are able to receive them.

The Great Invocation

"From the point of Light within the Mind of God
Let light stream forth into the minds of men.
Let Light descend on Earth.
From the point of Love within the Heart of God
Let love stream forth into the hearts of men.
May Christ return to Earth.
From the center where the Will of God is known
Let purpose guide the little wills of men
The purpose which the Masters know and serve.
From the center which we call the race of men
Let the Plan of Love and Light work out
And may it seal the door where evil dwells.
Let Light and Love and Power restore the Plan on Earth."

The invocation is a non-denominational prayer used by millions throughout the world. Transmission meditation an amazingly effective way of assisting humanity by drawing and receiving this energy. In the process of doing so your own energy is raised and developed.

The following is a quote from a flyer put out by TransmissionMeditation.org:

"No special expertise in meditation is required in order to transmit energy. All that is needed is alignment between the physical brain and the Soul. This is achieved by focusing the attention on the ajna center, the point between the eyebrows. If the attention wanders, gently sound OM and re-focus on that center. Do no mediate on the OM. All we are asked to do is maintain this alignment; the Masters do the work. Simplicity is the keynote."

"You may wish to establish a specific length of time for the transmission, e.g. one hour. Later it is recommended that the transmission continue until the energy flow ceases. Participants should feel free to leave whenever they wish, trying not to disturb those who are staying on. Group meetings adds an 'X' factor of potency to the work which is greater than can be achieved by individuals linking up mentally."

When silence is maintained with the focus on this ajna center it puts the meditator in a place of service. The individual then acts as a transmitter and conduit of higher energies coming into the Earth plane -- making them more accessible to others.

Tremendous energies are needed on the planet right now. Somw people aren't able to withstand these increased frequencies, as my professor had explained. For those who can't handle this higher frequency, behaviors may become erratic. Transmission Meditation allows a person to act as a "transmitter". You become a conduit for these energies to stream into the Earth plane, and you're also "stepping down" the frequencies so more people are able to access and handle these increased frequencies. There is a book on Transmission Meditation by Benjamin Creme (see Books and Resources).

The following chapters are different from what I've written so far. In the next chapters I'm sharing a few incidents in my life which help to illustrate the multi-faceted quality of existence; that there is much more to life than what we see. Please understand I'm definitely not any kind of a great example. Far from it! My life has been one of struggles and stupid mistakes. Yet for some reason it's also been one filled with unusual incidents. Hopefully what I share will help awaken an understanding of life's many layers and will pique your curiosity to explore these mysteries further.

18

A Harp Story

Spring was in the air and I was fifteen. The year was 1970 and I was just finishing sophomore year of high school. This summer a whole new world would open up for me.

In May of that year some posters around town caught my attention. They announced an introductory talk on Transcendental Meditation. It would be followed by lessons in meditation for anyone who was interested.

By 1970 I had a collection of metaphysical books. Ever since a near-death experience six years earlier I knew there was much more to life than what we see, and I was eager to read and learn all I could about the deeper meanings and purpose of life.

A year or so earlier I had read about the Beatles learning Transcendental Meditation from Maharishi Mahesh Yogi, and I was curious to know more about this method of opening your awareness. Those posters definitely caught my attention. I went to the lecture and as it turned out I was the only one in my home town that year who signed up to learn Transcendental Meditation afterward. At the time the student fee was only $25.

Meditation came very easily and naturally to me. It felt like I had done it forever. I was able to reach the states of silence right away, and soon my perceptions were getting sharper and sharper. Not long after I started meditating I became clairvoyant. At the time I thought it must happen that way for everyone who meditated, since the ability had come so easily. Later I found out this isn't true at all. I also learned certain foods, mellow or meditative music and even certain scents can facilitate this state for some people. Other substances can hinder or even block this heightened state of awareness. Unfortunately my clairvoyance was gone all too soon. I still have some of it, but not yet to the extent I once had.

I'll give you an example of what was possible for me back then. I could project my senses anywhere, with just the mere thought of something, no matter how distant it was. For example, if I was sitting in study hall and I wondered if there were cookies baking at home, somehow my sense of smell was projected to our kitchen at home by merely thinking of it. I could *smell* as well as *see* what was in the kitchen. If I wondered about getting mail that day then later, in the midst of whatever I was doing, I could *hear* the mail being dropped in the mailbox at home when the mailman came. I would also know if I received any mail and who had sent it to me.

I could ask myself anything, and I'd immediately know and fully understand the answer. It was amazing! I've learned since then that this ability, especially as quickly as it had come to me, is extremely rare though. It seldom happens like this for people when they start meditating. But meditation *does* help to sharpen your perceptions over time.

Later that summer Mom told me a great aunt was coming to town for a visit.

"I'm taking Aunt Marguerite to a little antique shop over by Otto's," she said. "Would you like to come with us?"

Aunt Marguerite was not one of our favorites, to put it politely. She was one of those older people who didn't like kids much. The fact *she* was going was all I needed to hear.

"No thanks!" I said and hurried off to do whatever I was doing. But as soon as I turned away I got the strong intuitive *knowing* there was something special *for me* at the little antique shop. I needed to go find it, whatever was essentially *mine* and waiting for me at the little shop. Much later I realized Mom's decision to go to this particular shop on that day was no coincidence.

My sixteenth birthday was coming soon, and I had received $25 in birthday cards from grandparents. So I ran up to my room and put the $25 in a little denim purse I had made. (I had embroidered birds in flight on that little purse. Over two and a half decades later, on my first trip to Egypt, I found those same birds in flight I would often draw in grade school. They were on the tiles of Akhenaten's summer palace and on walls at Saqqara.) Before long the three of us were on our way across town to the little antique shop.

We pulled up to an old white shingled house converted into a shop near some railroad tracks. We entered by a side door and I began my search immediately. It was like a treasure hunt. I methodically went around the store like a detective, inspecting each shelf and table while Mom and aunt Marguerite wandered around the store and chatted.

Eventually I had seen every item in the shop and I couldn't *believe* it! Nothing *told* me it was *for me*. I stood there confused and feeling something had to be *wrong*! Whatever it was *had to* be there! I *KNEW* it! The sense of knowing was a *certainty* -- not a maybe. Mom and Aunt Marguerite were leaving, and I just couldn't believe it! There *had to be* something there for me. I had felt it so clearly!

Just then, *at that very momen*t, a man walked through the door. An ambiance of mystery drifted into the shop with him. In his hand was an old, dusty and crumbling black cardboard box. It looked like it had been around forever. The box was about the size of a large briefcase. I stood there mesmerized, watching with fascination as this man walked quickly to the shop owner.

"Is *this* was what I came for?" I wondered. And at the same time I had the unmistakable sense it *was*. He set the box down and opened the lid. What lay inside this mysterious box was ancient, mythical-looking and lovely!

The man brushed his fingers across the top of this charming antique and immediately the dusty shop came alive with a magical sound. It was a tiny and very old *harp!* I was totally enchanted.

The wood was a rich mahogany color with gold highlights. At the top of the little harp was an image of old musical instruments done in ancient-looking gold tones and neutrals. I knew this was why I had come. I also knew I had to act swiftly. Before the man could say another word to the shop owner, I took a quick step forward.

"How much do you want for it?"

The man turned to this wide-eyed kid who he hadn't noticed before. He kind of had a twinkle in his eye and was obviously getting a kick out of this.

He grinned and answered slowly, "Oh... "

He paused, still looking at me and grinning. I stood there frozen, staring back at him in suspense -- wondering if I could possibly have enough money to buy this charming little harp. ...

" ... $25!" he said at last.

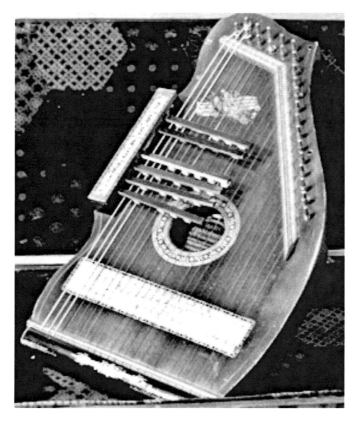

18a "Pianophone" zither harp from the antique store, 1970.

They were just the words I wanted to hear and I was elated! It was exactly what I had! I gladly handed him the money and took this little harp home.

I sat in my bedroom with this new treasure and carefully tuned the strings. Playing it came so naturally to me, as if I had played a harp all my life. The first thing I played was *Greensleeves*. The second was a tune I knew had been played in ancient Egypt. Funny, but I knew both tunes by heart. They were each from a very different faraway place and time, and yet they were tunes I was very familiar with, as if they had been a part of my life "forever".

As I played the Egyptian melody, I could *see* a parade of people walking up to the Great Pyramid in a diagonal line across the desert. This tune was being played on flutes and little harps, and I was at the head of the "parade". It was a fun and happy celebration.

There was something else I knew. I couldn't explain how, but I also knew this for a fact. A favorite friend of mine from a time in ancient Egypt had somehow *arranged* for this whole harp connection. This friend had influenced the entire scenario to happen. As strange as it may sound, I *knew* and sensed it all.

A friend from long ago had *arranged* for this little harp to be brought into the shop on that day and for me to be there just in time to buy it. Somehow I knew, as clearly as I knew my name, that this friend and I had both played harps in a time long ago and half a world away.

This little zither harp is an instrument unlike any others I've been able to find. The bars across it aren't played by pressing them. The notes plugged on the bars are the notes of the cords, and elastic at the end holds these bars in place. They are played by plucking the bars which creates   the sound of ancient chimes! There are seven bars, though one is missing in this photo. Inside the instrument it says "Pianophone".

164

Decades passed. In November 1999 I took my second of two trips to Egypt. A few days before we were to leave, totally out of the blue, I had an urge to bring a harp. I hadn't even played my little harp in years! But I had this urgent sense, for some strange reason, that I *needed* to take a little harp with me on this trip to Egypt.

In preparation for my trip I bought a new backpack, and I envisioned a little harp that would fit exactly inside it. This would be perfect! Whether or not a little harp that size even existed was another question altogether! It was something I would have to find out.

I didn't know why it suddenly felt so important. It was a silly idea, looking back on it, and we were leaving in a few days. But for some reason this is what I needed to do and I persisted against the odds in trying to find one. I called all the music stores in town and asked what stringed instruments they had.

The response was, "We have guitars, violins and a mandolin." Eventually, after days of calling music stores and getting similar responses I gave up. We would be leaving soon and I had so much to do.

Then something bizarre happened! The *very next day* after I had given up on ever finding a tiny harp, *TOTALLY OUT OF THE BLUE,* a catalog arrived in my mailbox! It was addressed to the previous resident, and it was amazing serendipity! The catalog was from a music store called Elderly Instruments in Lansing,

165

Michigan. And what did they have? A small harp that *happened* to fit *exactly* into my backpack! It was an astounding set of "coincidental" circumstances! And I was elated!

Years later I discovered that the little harp had been discontinued. It was no longer carried in the Elderly Instruments catalog. Such an amazing *coincidence* for it to be there just at the time when I needed it! And absolutely bizarre for the catalog to so mysteriously show up in my mailbox at just the right time! The entire incident was unforgettable.

After I had arrived in Cairo, on the night we were going inside the Great Pyramid, I told our American guide I had brought a little harp and said I'd like to play it inside the King's Chamber. His plan was to play recorded music inside the Chamber though. It was very strange, however, that his tape player would *not* play inside the pyramid! He tried for 20 minutes or so to get the tape player working, but it just wouldn't play although it worked fine outside the pyramid. In the end I didn't play the harp and we had no music at all inside the King's Chamber. I carried the little harp around in my backpack, playing it occasionally and briefly in a temple or special site.

Then one very special day we rode a boat along the Nile to see two temples that meant so much to me. They were the Philae Temple of Isis and the Edfu Temple of Horus, her son. The temples are situated not far from each other along the Nile. I was SO happy that day! For some reason those places were very important to me -- especially the temple of Horus. I felt an unexplained connection to Horus and Isis. It had been a great

166

disappointment that we didn't visit those temples on my first trip to Egypt two years earlier, so this was an extra special day. It felt like I was going to visit old friends, and I was so excited.

We visited Isis' temple of Philae first, and I loved it. I crawled thru a space there where I could *see* and *feel* having done it before long ago. I could *see* that long ago this little pit had been used for an initiation ceremony. At the time, it had been full of water and crocodiles or deadly animals. In an ancient time when I was going through the initiation ceremony, I made up my mind I had no reason to be afraid. I could *feel* once again the exhilarated sensation of rising above fear. Crawling through the pit on that day brought back all those elated feelings, as if it was yesterday. I felt the determined sense of courage and the triumph of making it successfully through the ceremony with absolutely no fear so long ago.

Later, as we were leaving Philae and waiting for everyone to gather and board the boat, I got out my little harp and began to play. Our sweet Egyptian guide Emil Shaker saw me playing and went absolutely ballistic! He stared at me with his mouth wide open in a look of shocked disbelief.

"You play the **Harp**?" he asked excitedly, as if he had just seen a ghost or something.

"I've been trying for *months* to find a musician for this *very day!*" Emil was so excited he was shouting now. He stood there looking absolutely shocked that I played a harp and had brought one with me.

"For *months* I called and called musicians, one after the other!" he said. I could feel the desperation in his voice of trying in vain to find a musician for that very day. "And *none* of them could play today! Finally, at the last minute, I found two who said they could perform. But they cancelled, one after the other"

Emil was still staring wide-eyed, with a look of total astonishment on his face. He went on to explain that the Philae Temple of Isis had been moved, stone by stone, to its current location. The Aswan Dam, built between 1960 and 1970, had flooded its original location. Emil had wanted so desperately for us to go out on the Nile when we left the Philae temple, and to stop the boat over the original location where it had once stood. He wanted to say a prayer-like tribute and then have a musician play something in memory of Isis and her original temple.

"And do you know what Isis played?!" Emil was still shouting and staring at me in disbelief. "Isis played the **Harp**!"

The words seemed to grab my heart. A flood of feelings swept through me and I felt a surge of emotion. It was such a moving moment on this day. Isis played the harp! I felt honored and grateful for this all to have fallen into place. I could play my little harp in dedication to Isis on that day.

18b Horus and I at Edfu temple, Dec. 1999

We got into the boat, sailed out a little way across the Nile and the boat hovered over the spot where the Isis temple once stood. We said a tribute to Isis and I let my fingers play across the strings of the little harp. The music sounded very ancient, and also very Egyptian.

Afterward some of the girls came up to me and asked excitedly, "Did you know you were channeling Isis?!" I don't know exactly what was happening there, but it's a memory I'll always keep close. From there we went to the Edfu temple of Horus, which I had been wanting for years to visit.

I walked through those rooms feeling suspended in time. A strange longing sensation would always surge through me whenever I would see pictures of the Horus falcon. The chance to visit his temple on this trip was incredibly exciting. I'd also get to stand beside the Horus statue and to touch it.

I now have a lovely 30" Celtic harp, which I got from BlevinsHarps.com. It's a Bouree 26 in natural walnut with a rich figured grain. The sound is amazing, and it was actually an interesting string of synchronicities or "coincidences" that led me to find it. The synchronicities continue to go on.

(I also have a lovely 23" native American flute in G from Douglas Blue Feather, as well as a smaller 17.5" B flute. Both were made by High Spirits Flutes out of lovely aromatic Cedar. Their wide diameter or *bore* gives them incredible rich deep tones! Interestingly, Cedar is a wood with mysterious legends, known for particularly high energy. It is the only element mentioned in the Bible over 200 times. King Solomon traded two cities for enough Cedar to line the temple that once held the Arc of the Covenant because the wood was known to have such a high level of energy.)

19

Experiences in Egypt

My first trip was in November 1997. However the whole Egypt experience began with a mysterious little incident two years earlier. One day in 1995 a brochure advertising a trip to Egypt showed up in my mailbox. It was a glossy fold-out with pictures of sacred sites, including the Valley of the Kings. Nice images, but it was junk mail. I was *so* far from being able to afford or even think about a trip to Egypt! I was going to toss it right in the trash, but when I walked through my doorway for some reason I couldn't throw the brochure away. I dropped it on the coffee table instead.

Later that night when I was going to bed this brochure caught my eye, and I brought it into the bedroom with me. For a few moments I sat on the bed looking at the lovely images of Egypt before going to sleep. What happened next is still vivid in my mind as though it was yesterday.

After looking at the scenes of Egypt, I put the brochure on my night stand, turned out the lamp and lay down to sleep. As soon as I closed my eyes and my head hit the pillow the strangest thing happened! I was still very much awake but found myself immediately "transported" thousands of miles away and thousands of years back in time. I found myself "waking up" inside a cave-like setting where I was on a stone slab-type platform.

It was all strangely so real! I sat up and looked around to see where I was and found I was in a type of stone "room". I stood and walked over to a crude opening in the rock and looked out. A few yards in front of me was a high cliff with an undulating surface. I was looking at it from the vantage point of being high above the ground inside another rock formation facing that cliff. I could then see I was several yards up from ground level.

To my left the cliffs joined each other in a cul-de-sac type u formation of cliffs. When I looked off to my right what I saw was the Valley of the Kings.

Two years later a series of *coincidences* happened which led to my being able to take a trip to Egypt. I *happened* to come into the house at exactly the right moment and turned on the TV to the right station. At that moment a noon news anchor announced QVC was looking for unique items from each state. I got the QVC phone number, found out about the program, and sent some photos of jewelry I was making. They ended up placing an order for a thousand necklaces! This good fortune made my first trip to Egypt possible.

There were many unusual circumstances running through each of my two trips to Egypt. From the very beginning, each trip was prefaced with a catastrophic event happening just a few days before we were to leave. Both events involved Egypt and it was a strange *coincidence* for this to happen both times, just a few days before each trip.

In November 1997 three days before we were to leave on the first trip the world was rocked with the Massacre at Hatshepsut's Tomb. It was a horrible event covered by CNN 24/7. The news detailed the brutal torture inflicted on the Japanese tourists at the site. This created an atmosphere of fear and groups around the world cancelled their trips to Egypt. For some reason our group was still going though, amidst all this fear and uncertainty.

Throughout those three days leading up to my trip, friends and family would call me at least 6 or 7 times a day with gruesome details of the tortures and killings. They pleaded and tried to scare me into canceling my trip. I was so torn between longing to go and the uncertainty of it being safe. To help me determine what to do I called the State Department in Washington D.C. The security specialist I spoke to kind of laughed it off. I had guessed they must be accustomed to these circumstances. He said it was the safest time to go because security would be especially tight.

It was all I needed to hear! So against the threats and looming fears, I boarded a plane in Detroit heading for New York City. Once there I'd connect with a group of people I had never met before and travel to this faraway and possibly hostile country. Despite my resolve to go, the uncertainty still lingered. I couldn't help but wonder as I took my seat in Detroit if I had made a terrible mistake.

To get my mind on other thoughts I got out my little sketchbook and the small *Traveler's Guide to Egypt* I had brought along. I opened the book to a statue of Akhenaten and started sketching. Immediately the tall man sitting to my left in the aisle seat looked at what I was doing and a startled look seemed to explode across his face.

"You going to Egypt?" he said with a heavy accent and a priceless look of astonishment.

I hadn't really noticed the man much until then. He was tall with a dark complexion, and as friendly as could be.

Of all things! Of all planes, and of all seats! I could hardly believe this stroke of *fate*. The man sitting beside me *happened* to be from Cairo! On an ordinary flight from Detroit to New York, he *happened* to be sitting right next to me and I was connecting in New York to fly to Cairo! What a funny *coincidence*! He swept the fear and uncertainty right out of my mind, and set my trip out on a positive, upbeat note!

The man told me he was an engineer on Mount Sinai. This was another interesting twist, because climbing Mount Sinai was a highlight of my trip. His smile and attitude were exceptionally

174

welcoming. He assured me I would find the Egyptian people very kind and that they will be friendly and happy to see our group.

In that moment all my worries and concerns just slipped away. They were all transformed to happiness and excitement about my coming adventure. And the man was totally right! The trip and the people turned out to be wonderful! ... Thinking back as I write this, I can't help but wonder a little about the identity of that man...

In New York I met up with others in the group and boarded an Egypt Air flight into Cairo. I sat in a window seat forward of the wing on the left side. This would later turn out to be a great advantage.

As the plane swept across the Mediterranean Sea, I was practically soaring out of my skin with excitement! It felt like I was riding on the back of some huge antediluvian bird, swooping in across the ancient sea. Europe was there on the left and the continent of Africa on my right. The sky on the right was blazing with drama and intense colors as the sun was setting. The atmosphere was breathlessly magical, and it exactly matched my soaring excitement! I will never forget this welcome to the Mediterranean. It was like entering another world.

We approached Cairo in total darkness. The pilot made a sweeping dip beside the Giza Plateau on our left, and golden images pierced dramatically through the darkness. The Pyramids and Sphinx glowed golden through the black background. What a magnificent welcome into Cairo! And I had the perfect seat for the view.

When we arrived at the hotel, I dropped my bags in the room and went out on the balcony. Egypt was calling and I couldn't wait to immerse myself in the experience. What met my eyes took my breath away.

The Great Pyramid stood *right there* in front of me! This imposing megalithic structure was *right there*! And the opening on its side was beckoning. It was extraordinary! I had no idea our hotel was *so* close to the Giza Plateau. It turned out we were staying at the nicest hotel in town -- the Mena House Oberoi Hotel, which is a magnificent converted palace. It's on what was once the outskirts of Cairo. The city now actually sprawls out to meet it. This hotel is situated right at the base of the Giza Plateau.

Standing on that balcony, breathing in the Cairo air and lost somewhere in another time, I clearly heard a voice say, "Welcome! We've been waiting for you!" It startled me from my trance-like state, and left a lingering question in my mind. I wondered just who the "We" is...

On that first day we walked up to the Giza Plateau. What an experience! We were the only ones on that magnificent plateau. It was just our group, those awesome monuments, and the ancient Sahara sands. Later a CNN crew showed up and interviewed us on the Plateau, since we were the only tourists in Egypt at the time.

We stood for a few moments in front of the smaller pyramid of Khafre and a flood of memories came rushing over me. I had walked up beside that pyramid before! I was in a long line of people trailing across the Sahara in a diagonal line from the southeast up to the Giza Plateau. It was a type of parade. The memory was so vivid, as if I was remembering an incident from just a few years earlier.

Images of that "parade" were *so* real. I could *see* and *feel* it all again, as if it had just taken place the day before. In a faraway time I was in a happy line of people making its way across the desert to the Giza Plateau. Both flutes and harps were being played. The melody was the one I had played on the little zither harp -- the one I found twenty-seven years earlier at the antique shop.

Still, in a way it seemed strange to me. "Parades" in ancient Egypt seemed so unlikely. I had to know if it was really true -- if this really could have happened back then.

"Did they have *parades* in ancient Egypt?", I asked our Egyptian guide Emil (see Resources and Books). He stared at me for a few moments in silence. I was anxious to know his thoughts, but I couldn't read Emil's surprised expression, and it felt like I was using the wrong word.

"What's another name for parade?" I asked, groping for the right word. After a few moments someone in the group called out,

177

"procession." I then looked back at Emil and asked this question. I had to know the answer.

"Did they have *processions* in ancient Egypt?" Emil looked at me again with a blank, surprised stare. Then came a statement that left me hanging. It didn't answer my question.

"**_You_** tell **_me_**!" was Emil's enigmatic answer.

I looked back across the desert and again could *see* that procession happening. I could *hear* the musicians, and I felt the excitement I was feeling at the time as we approached the Giza Plateau and the pyramids. As I stood there remembering this whole scene, I could hear Emil talking to a man beside him. He spoke slowly and in a hushed tone.

"Royalty used to live across the desert, in that direction, thousands of years ago", he said.

The massacre at Hatshepsut's Tomb, in a strange twist, would be a tremendous advantage for us. It would end up making our trip extra special. As a result of the catastrophe, Egypt and those wonderful ancient sites were free of tourists. Those temples and palaces were absolutely, majestically silent as we entered them. The serenity allowed us to be completely immersed the sacred sites. We could experience each place without the distractions of the usual crowds of tourists. When you enter such a powerful place in total silence, qualities of the time when it was built seem to come alive and surge through you. I could actually *feel* how those sites had been long ago in ancient times.

We were told that normally Egypt is so crowded with tourists it is almost like an amusement park atmosphere. There are tourists everywhere talking, munching, taking pictures and asking you to take their pictures. The rare circumstances surrounding our trip created an extraordinary opportunity for us. We could experience the country in all its native splendor.

As the days progressed and we visited temples and historic sites daily, I learned that there indeed _were_ processions in ancient Egypt. They would consist mostly of royalty and would travel to temples and pyramids for special sacred ceremonies.

When we arrived in the Valley of the Kings I wanted to look for the tomb where two years earlier I had felt transported. Unfortunately I didn't have the chance to find that tomb. It didn't fit into the schedule of our American guide. His days were already planned.

The Valley of the Kings is *much* larger than I had imagined. There are nooks or cul-de-sac type configurations of undulating cliffs *everywhere,* and it's a huge area! I sensed that there would be a right time in the future. What I also sensed is there would be a time when I would return to Egypt and I would find that tomb.

Two years later I again had the opportunity to go to Egypt. As I was making plans for the trip, thoughts of the catastrophe just days before the last trip came to mind. And then I had this momentary thought. I wondered whether an incident would happen to create similar conditions where the country would be free of crowds of visitors. I didn't want another catastrophe, but I couldn't help but wonder if this circumstance would somehow repeat itself.

Unlikely as it was, just days before we were to leave for this second trip to Egypt in November of 1999, guess what happened? Egypt Air crashed. It was the same scenario all over again! As before, the group I was traveling with (Power Places Tours) didn't cancel, although other groups and tourists around the world had canceled their trips. When I connected with the group in New York, our guide wouldn't leave the airport until they changed the number of our flight from the now infamous one that had just crashed. It was quite an ordeal.

Again the plane swooped in beside the Giza Plateau on the left. This time I arranged to sit on the left to prepare for that breathtaking view. The trip was wonderful, and being there again felt absolutely fantastic.

We took the overnight train to southern Egypt and visited the ancient Temple of Seti I at Abydos. This time we also visited the older ruins behind the Seti Temple called the Osirian. It was still being excavated and was flooded, so we couldn't enter. After seeing the Osirian ruins, we returned across the desert and back through the Seti temple to return to our hotel.

I happened to be the first one to enter the Seti temple's dark hallway at the back entrance. It was the strangest thing! As I took a step through that passageway, a beam of light shot in above my right shoulder. *Whoosh!* Like a bolt of lightning, this beam of light shot into the dark hallway and fell across an image on the left wall just ahead of me. Suddenly the hand of Osiris holding the sacred rods of Initiation seemed to leap out of the darkness, boldly announcing its presence.

19a Hand of Osiris holding the sacred rods at the Seti I temple.

It was one more incident that took my breath away. Not wanting to make a big deal of it, I silently took a picture as I walked by before continuing on through the temple.

Years afterward I realized this was a "repeat" of a similar scenario that had happened two years earlier. Several of the elements were the same.

During that first trip to Egypt two years earlier, we visited a special temple behind Karnak in Luxor. This was another very special temple and again I happened to be the first one into a very dark room. It was a small room devoted to Sekhmet. I walked right up to the statue of Sekhmet and put my hands on her hands which were holding those same sacred rods. It just felt right at the time. The group had a little tribute ceremony to Sekhmet and as soon as we finished Emil had climbed up on the roof and removed a brick covering a hole in the far corner of the room. Immediately a beam of light shot in and bolted across Sekhmet's hands which held the rods of Initiation. My hands were also in the path of the beam of light that time.

Not long after visiting the Osirian on the later second trip we went to the Valley of the Kings. This time we took a different path from the one taken two years earlier. The next event is still a mystery to me. While walking up a certain path in the Valley, suddenly I found myself frozen in my tracks. I stood there in disbelief! Ahead of me was that *VERY* formation of undulating cliffs I had *seen* in the experience from my bedroom four years earlier!

When I got over the initial shock, I immediately whipped around to see "the tomb" cliff facing it. Sure enough! There was the other cliff facing the first one! It was the exact distance away as I had experienced it four years earlier. This was the astounding part though. A massive manmade stone stands in front of that cliff, guarding it.

I've never seen a stone like it anywhere else in Egypt! It resembles a *HUGE* tombstone, with perfectly straight sides. Most striking is the top of that monolithic stone. It's shaped in a pointed dome, resembling the Taj Mahal. The stone has a dramatic impact, and there is nothing like it anywhere else in the Valley. It's hard to believe that no one has pointed out this mysterious monolithic stone. Obviously the time hasn't come yet to reveal what this stone is guarding.

"This is it! This is *the cliff!*" I called to our American guide. I had mentioned both two years earlier and that morning how I would love to find the cliff I had experienced four years earlier.

As the tour guide, he had other things to think about though and he had scheduled one last tomb to visit. He told me that I could go up there to investigate it if I wanted, but that the last bus would be leaving soon and the Valley of the Kings would be closing for the day. He said I could spend the night out there alone if I wanted to, but that everyone else would be gone.

Once again I knew the time wasn't right. It was such an immense disappointment this time though, because I had actually FOUND the tomb! And what stood in front of it was *amazing*. But I also knew it still wasn't the right time for this discovery to be made. I knew there would be another time in the future when this tomb would reveal its secrets.

20

Clues to the

Egyptian Mysteries

In the years since those Egyptian experiences, incidents continued to happen that would validate them. Other "chance" meetings and events added new meaning to the Egyptian thread running through my life.

In the late 1990s, I first heard of Remote Viewing. It's a method of training and using one's intuitive abilities. In the following years I read several books to learn more about it. These included *Psychic Warrior* by David Morehouse, *Remote Perceptions* by Angela Thompson, *The Ultimate Time Machine* by Joe McMoneagle and Charles T. Tart, *Remote Viewers: The Secret History of America's Psychic Spies* by Jim Schnabel, and *Captain Of My Ship, Master Of My Soul* by F. Holmes (Skip) Atwater. Other books have since been added to that list.

Remote Viewing began as a United States government program to train psychic spies. The protocols for Remote Viewing had been developed by Ingo Swann. It utilizes the mind's latent capacities to *know, see* and in any way *perceive* at a distance. This ability is otherwise known as *nonlocal* perception. Among other applications, Remote Viewing is used to solve crimes, find lost children, and in other ways to benefit individuals and society.

Over the years I've ended up meeting several of the original remote viewers, some of whom I consider friends. In 2003 I met Stephan Schwartz. He has been interested in how extraordinary human functioning can affect social change. One of his strong interests has been using intuitive abilities in archaeology.

The books *The Secret Vaults of Time: Psychic Archaeology and the Quest for Man's Beginnings*, and *The Alexandria Project* by Stephan Schwartz are fascinating accounts of how researchers have successfully located archaeological sites using Remote Viewing. One of the chief research team members was a gifted Canadian man named George McMullen.

George had strong intuitive abilities all his life, and he had a particularly strong connection with the earth. His ability to locate and describe elements in the earth proved to be an invaluable skill. See the books and recommendations pages for George's books. *One White Crow* tells of his experiences working with Canadian archaeologist Dr. Norman Emerson. See also http://archived.parapsych.org/psychic_archeology.htm Other books give interesting accounts of other lives and figures in history from the perspective of Native American spirits present on the land.

20a George McMullen holding a Mayan artifact on the balcony of his oceanfront home (his last home) in White Rock, BC, Canada.

Archaeologists as well as companies needing to dig for artifacts, ore or minerals would seek out George for his ability. George would visit an area where he would pace across the ground to get a *feel* for it. He would then give what he called an "intuitive survey", pinpointing the exact location where the desired items were located. His survey would also include highly detailed information on what was to be found and exactly where and how deep those items or minerals would be located. I was excited to hear about George. His skill intrigued me and most importantly, I had been living with a great mystery for years; the mystery of just what was inside that tomb in the Valley of the Kings.

I knew George was getting old, and didn't know if it was even right to bother him with this question. So I emailed Stephan, explaining the mystery and asking if he thought it would be all right to ask for George's help. Stephan gave me the "go ahead", along with George's email address. I emailed George in early 2007 giving a detailed description of the tomb I had found and its location. George responded that he had received the email, but then I didn't hear anything further. Because of his age and health issues, I didn't want to push it.

Later that year I was excited to discover George would be a speaker at the International Remote Viewing Conference (IRVA) in the fall. It would be the second year in a row George would be a speaker at the IRVA Conference. I knew perhaps this would be my *only* chance to meet him. George was then 87. So I excitedly made plans to attend the Conference in October 2007. Meeting George McMullen and Wayne Peterson were the highlights of that unforgettable weekend.

This was an interesting connection having to do with George McMullen at the Conference. I had been asked ahead of time if I'd design and donate jewelry for the IRVA bidding table. I wanted to design jewelry that was unique, and thoughts of one very special bead came to mind. It was a 2,000 year-old Mayan pottery bead. I used this along with Lapis Lazuli and Copal Amber I bought in the Himalayas of Nepal. I also incorporated unique gemstones, artifacts and ethnic beads.

What was interesting is that it "just so happened" George was speaking on ancient Native American artifacts at the Conference!

20b Artifact necklace, shown in color at ExploringSacredSpace.com

I discovered this after I got there. He had brought a case filled with the same type of ancient Native American pottery beads from North, Central and South America. His weren't as old as mine, but it was an interesting "coincidence" that I had chosen to use the Mayan pottery bead artifact for this Conference where George had similar artifacts on display.

George was captivated with the necklace I had made, and he ended up winning the bid on it! Thanks, that is, to Eric Lash who had actually won the bid. George was an active bidder and thought he had made the final winning bid. He was devastated to discover he hadn't won it after all. Realizing how disappointed George was, Eric kindly let George bid $1 more to win the necklace. George then gave the jewelry as a gift to Diane Dyann, his Business Manager. Diane has also been a great help with the final editing of this book.

At the Conference, a crowd of people had gone to George's suite Friday evening. I only found out about it the next day, with a sense of disappointment. On Saturday I planned to meet and speak to George somehow. When the lectures concluded in the evening I went to his suite. Only three other people were there that night, in addition to Diane. It was perfect!

I sat right next to George and introduced myself as the one who had emailed about the Egyptian tomb experience. George's warm eyes flashed a spark of recollection. With the warmth of a wise grandfather, George told me about the tomb. He explained with a sense of certainty, "*That tomb* was built for the daughters of Seti."

"So they are inside this tomb?" I asked, wanting to be certain.

"Yes", George verified.

Seti was the pharaoh who built the Osirian temple. It was erected at the site where the head of Osiris was believed to have been buried many centuries earlier. The ground was considered sacred for that reason. I sat there in awe of his statement. It certainly cast a new "light" on the beam that shot in over my right shoulder as I entered the Osirian in 1999. It also helped to explain why the place seemed so familiar to me. And yet, there was an echoing sense I *hadn't* been one of Seti's daughters . . .

Another memory gripped my heart when I heard this. It was a recollection burned inside of me as if it were part of my childhood and part of my life. The memory and its location became clearer after I first visited the Osirian in 1977. I would sometimes get clear memories of being a small child in ancient Egypt and playing on the ground along an outer wall of the Osirian. I'd play with other children, using stones kind of like marbles.

Every day, like clockwork, a servant would interrupt our play to bring me inside. There was something I needed to do. It was my duty. We'd enter the Osirian and walk down a long passageway. We'd turn right into a secluded dark hallway, and take one more right into a small special room. The room was placed off a series of turns so no light from the outside would enter. The room was a special and secluded sanctuary.

One lit candle on a tall golden candlestick cast a warm glow throughout the little room. The candle was on the other side of a highly decorated golden chair. I'd enter the room and after I was seated in the chair the servant would leave. I can still *see* her taking one last look at me from the doorway before leaving and heading back down that hallway. Meditating in this room was a daily ritual. It was my duty to become clairvoyant. This was the method, which began in early childhood, to train intuitive abilities. On my trips to Egypt I noticed many of the temples had a secluded small room with very brilliant images on the walls. The images hadn't been faded by the sun over the years. I realized those were the rooms devoted to meditation and opening one's potential abilities.

Months later I had a phone reading with Kevin Ryerson. He's a gifted clairvoyant who had been discussed in Shirley MacLaine's *Out On A Limb*. Wayne Peterson had suggested that I have a reading with Kevin to learn about some of my past lives. Kevin Ryerson's readings are like channelings. He has several different personalities who come through him to give the readings. One of them is an Egyptian, and this was the personality who came through for my reading. The information I was given turned out to be more pieces of the puzzle in understanding my Egyptian connections over the years,.

"You were raised in the Osirian from childhood on", said a deep voice with an Egyptian accent. "You were raised to be a priestess who was in charge of Seti's daughters."

A flood of images and feelings coursed through me. I now had more of an understanding of mysteries that had filled my life. No wonder *The Search for Om Sety* by Jonathan Cott seemed so familiar to me. It's the biographical novel of Dorothy Eady's life. She remembered having been Seti's wife and living in the Osirian in ancient times. She went to live in Egypt to be close to the Osirian. Egyptians accepted Dorothy as the former wife of Seti.

Thoughts of Elisabeth Haich's book *Initiation* also came to mind. Werner had recommended the book, and I read it in the 1970s. It gives the fascinating account of Elisabeth's former life as a priestess for Ptahhotep in Saqqara, which is not far from Cairo. Ptahhotep was a pharaoh of the fifth dynasty.

I hesitated adding this chapter. I have only done it at the recommendation of others because these incidents are more pieces of the puzzle which help to explain other occurrences.

George McMullen passed away June 4, 2008.

21

A Pre-Destined Crystal

The details of this incident still amaze me. It reveals there is much more to life than what we see.

In the late '60s, people began wearing crystal pendants. I've always loved natural stones, and in grade school I started a little rock collection. So of course I wanted a crystal pendant. Something strange would happen, however, if I ever went to buy one. I would get a strong intuitive sense that I was *not* to buy one ... that someday I would find *my crystal*. Funny as it may sound, I knew *I wasn't to buy a crystal until I found mine*, because no other crystal would be the right energy match.

So for years I'd look at crystal pendants if I saw them in shops, but none ever "told me" they were for me. Over a decade passed and I still hadn't found my crystal.

Then in 1983, I was teaching in Hawaii. While there I had met a wonderful man named Reg Newbon who taught Healing classes. That fall I had taken a workshop with Reg on the Big Island. During Easter break 1984 I flew to California to do another workshop with him.

The workshop was on a very special hill called Paraiso Hot Springs, south of San Jose. I flew to San Francisco, spent a few nights with a cousin there, and then took a bus south. Reg picked me up at a small bus station and we drove for miles across the flat open desert.

Suddenly ahead of us a wonderful hill rose in the midst of the flat desert. It looked quite out of place -- like an illustration in a children's fairy tale book! We got closer and the energy was *tremendously* uplifting and intense! When we reached this "magical" hill, the road going up it was lined on both sides with the TALLEST, most *regal* Palm trees I have ever seen! They created an effect of lifting our spirits to the heights as we ascended this hill. The experience was incredible! The whole weekend was a cascade of exhilarating experiences. I will mention a few highlights of that weekend.

We reached the top of this powerful hill and met up with all the others. After finding our rooms, Reg took us to a special location in the woods. He had chosen this spot for a sacred Medicine Wheel to begin our weekend. A Medicine Wheel is a circle blessed with special intentions. It brings heightened energy and a quality of blessing and sacredness to a place.

We sat around a fire in this Medicine Wheel space which Reg had encircled with stones, and Reg said a blessing. After the blessing we meditated for a little while. When I closed my eyes to meditate I found myself "transported" to the distant past. What I *saw* were very serene people in long peach robes performing a ceremony. I knew these were priests who lived on this piece of land in the far distant past, and I was seeing them perform a sacred ceremony on this very spot.

We came out of meditation and Reg spoke -- in his wonderful soft yet strong voice with a soothing British accent. (He was originally from England, though he has lived in America for decades now. (Presently he has a center called Capstone in Boulder City, California.)

"This special mountain has always been sacred", Reg said. "In the distant past it was part of Lemuria. It was a separate island where priests lived and held special ceremonies." Then he added, "The vibrational color of this spot is orange".

So it was *Lemurian* priests I had seen! And they wore robes of a soft orange reflecting the vibratory color of the place. What I also felt was that this vibratory color orange came to be associated as a sacred color among other Asian groups. Over time the shade reflected less and less light, becoming a deeper tone of orange, it seemed, as mankind's consciousness became more and more dense.

194

On Easter Sunday I was the first to wake up. This moment is still *a* vivid memory. It was an incredibly breathtaking experience. I went outside on this Easter morning when the world was still asleep, and my breath was literally taken away!

21a Sunrise above the clouds, Paraiso Hot Springs, Easter 1984.

Our sacred little mountain was *surrounded* with *CLOUDS!* We were *above* the clouds! It's one of those moments when you *had to be there* to feel the specialness of that moment. It felt like I was in heaven!

In the picture the gray area between the black silhouette of the foliage is *clouds*! You can also see some of those regally *tall* palm trees. The sky immediately above the gray cloud area is the most magnificent shade of peach fading into violet. And, you can hardly see this here, but in the lower left nook rising from the gray cloud and black foliage area is the edge of *THE SUN!* The Sun was *rising above the clouds!* Totally breathtaking! Like being part of a sunrise in Heaven.

At that workshop I was also captivated by something else. For the *first time* since the late '60s when people first began wearing crystal pendants, I saw two crystal pendants that blew me away! There was such immense energy from those crystals. I was elated! At last I had found my crystal maker! I was so excited.

There was a guy and a woman who each wore one of these crystals. They lived hundreds of miles apart, but they had each managed to find a crystal of exceptional energy. It turned out they were both made by the same man.

"*WHERE* did you get your crystal?" I asked the woman with the surprised curiosity of a kid at Christmas. "And who made it? I want to have one made by this person!"

Her response was a complete *low* to the *high* of my excitement.

"Oh, I'm sorry!" she said casually. "You can't get a crystal made by this man. They were made by a Native American who lives in a remote reservation inside the Grand Canyon. He has no phone and there's no way to reach him. He only brings one or two crystals to a random shop once in a while, but the shop could be anywhere and in any state. Crystals made by this man are next to impossible to find. Sorry. You won't be able to get one made by him, but maybe you could find one similar to these", she said with a smile.

Their crystals were each long and very slender. They also each had a different colored stone set on top set in gold. It wasn't the shape or the colored stones that was so compelling to me. It was the *feeling and energy* those crystals had. I knew it all had to do with the man who had made the pendants. And I wanted one made by this man.

Her negative response only dampened my enthusiasm slightly. I had *such* an immense feeling that I had at last found the maker of "my crystal"! Her words brought a sense of disappointment for sure, but something inside of me knew I had *found* the maker of my crystal.

She told me the name of this man. It's a name I no longer remember -- but at the time the name was burned into my memory. Somehow I'd find a crystal made by this man. Or was it the other way around? Maybe it was *the crystal* that would *find me*...

After the workshop I went back to San Francisco and spent a couple nights with a cousin there before catching my flight back to Hawaii. The day after I arrived, when my cousin Rob went to work, I got out the San Francisco phone book. I turned to the *Yellow Pages* and looked up "Rock Shops". In 1984 there were *columns* and *pages* of Rock Shops in the San Francisco phone book -- dozens, if not *hundreds* of them! I remember that day clearly. And I can *see* the phone book. I randomly chose a place from the upper center column of the right hand page and called the shop. I found out where they were and which buses I'd have to take to get there.

It turned out to be quite a distance away -- now that I think of it! It wasn't the closest or most convenient shop for sure -- but for some reason it was the only one I felt the impulse to visit. I had to take two buses to get there. The bus finally dropped me off at a strip of shops in an old building with one of those tall western facades. The shop was set up like a small jewelry store. All the gemstones were behind glass in locked cases. I looked around but saw no pendants! They were mostly large rocks, geodes and some smaller more precious stones.

"May I help you?" a man asked.

"Yes! I'm looking for a crystal pendant", I said with a smile.

"Oh, I'm sorry! We have no pendants at all!"

I stood there for a moment feeling stunned. Why hadn't I asked over the phone if they even *had* pendants?! I got all the way out there on my *ONE day* in San Francisco! And they don't even *have pendants*! I could hardly believe it. It felt like I had just been dropped from on high out of a hot air balloon. It was *such* a tremendous let down! But I "picked myself up" and decided to make the most of my day. I walked around the shop looking at all the lovely rocks before catching a bus back to my cousin's place.

Heading for the door, I stopped one more time to look at the free-standing circular glass case. And I was *amazed* at what was staring back at me! *There* in the center of the case, on a tiny pedestal, was something I hadn't seen before! There was *a quartz pendant set in gold*!

"Excuse me!" My voice had an excited tone of urgency. "I'd like to see something in this case please!"

So the man comes over and as he gets closer he sees the pendant. "Oh *that!*" he says in a moment of recollection. "I forgot! A little Indian guy was in a few days ago and left that."

21b The crystal set in gold with gold wire wrapped on top for strength.

He said the name, and it was *that guy*! My jaw dropped! Of all things! I was amazed at all the serendipity of my finding that crystal, or it finding _me_. It was like finding a "needle in a haystack" in San Francisco! And I understood the whole situation! This man was so intuitive that, whether consciously or subconsciously, he connected with the person who would own each pendant as he was making them. He would not only choose the perfect stone for that person, he also perceived exactly when and where to bring it so their paths would cross! Amazing!

The two people I had seen at the workshop wore very slender crystals and each one had a different colored stone set at the top. Their crystals "matched" them perfectly. My crystal is shorter and wider, with a different quality of energy. I've recently seen this type of crystal in Katrina Raphael's *Crystal Healing* book. It has a large front face that has seven sides with a triangle shaped smaller face on the opposite side. It's called a "channeling crystal". A crystal in this particular formation is rare. The book states that some "channeling crystals" have been programmed by ancient elders and those crystals are for particular people who will attract them into their lives. They're not necessarily used for "channeling", but are for channeling spiritual energy and the light of wisdom into your being. The book states they're also for receiving vast information and that they will "find" their owners. I'm smiling as I write this. Like the little harp, it feels like a "'treasure" destined to be mine.

There are many good books that give the energy qualities of crystals. "The Book of Stones: Who They Are and What They

Teach" by Robert Simmons and Naisha Ahsian is particularly good because it's a large size and shows color pictures of each stone along with the description and energies of each. Judy Hall also has two small books with color pictures and descriptions of each stone. They are "The Crystal Bible" and "The Crystal Bible 2".

Katrina Raphael has a trilogy of Crystal books that give both the spiritual qualities of stones as well as instructions for healing methods using the stones. I've listed them in Resources and Books at the end of this book. Once of my new favorites is "The American Indian Secrets Of Crystal Healing" by Luc Bourgault. I love to hear what the native Americans sense from the gemstones because they have a natural intuitive knowing about things of the Earth. Another very interesting book is "Gems and Stones". It only lists twenty-two gems, stones and metals, but it gives the direct healing and spiritual qualities of them from the readings of Edgar Cayce.

22

The

Maltese Connection

It's an interesting story how Ari, my Maltese pooch, and I found each other. One day in November 1998 while in meditation, an image of a small white pup appeared in my mind. At the time I had no idea who my pup would be, though I had been looking for *my pup* for many months. Five months later I found him and realized I had *seen* this very pup while in meditation on the day he had been born back in November.

This is how we found each other. In March of 1999, on the anniversary of the death of the two-pound Yorkie I'd watch for months at a time while its owners traveled the world buying gemstones, this is what happened. I woke up that morning and looked sadly at the spot on the floor where I had found this sweet little dog dead a year earlier.

The previous year, when its owners had brought the Yorkie to my house, I "heard" the words, "This dog is going to die tonight." I quickly put those words out of my mind, but I woke the next morning horrified to find her dead beside my bed. It was an incredibly sad day. So on that day one year later when I woke up I sadly thought of the sweet Yorkie.

I got up and brought the paper in to look in the classifieds for a Maltese. I had been looking for a Maltese for many months, but couldn't find either a breeder or anybody even selling one. On that morning in 1999, for the first time in a year, there was a Maltese advertised for sale under *Pets* in the classifieds!

In preparation for my dog, I had already decided to name it after my trip to Egypt. By that time I had already bought a book of Egyptian names. I had chosen the name Ari, which was the name of an ancient Egyptian Fire god. It means "Light" in the Arab/ Egyptian languages.

This was another one of those bizarre *coincidences*. I dialed the number advertising the Maltese on that day in March of 1999 and the woman answered, "Arianna's Kennel!"

When I arrived at the breeder's she showed me his papers. More serendipity! I was amazed to read that his mother's name was *Ariel*, and had been *born on the one-year anniversary of my first trip to Egypt!* And then I discovered the Maltese breed is from the island of Malta, north of Alexandria, Egypt. It was a breed favored by Egyptian royalty, who often owned these dogs.

22a I call this photo "The Little Buddha" because he's on a Tibetan prayer rug.

It definitely seemed like a connection that was meant to be. For some reason this little dog was meant to be mine.

23

The Spring

Full Moon Festivals

There are three major high-points of the year known as the Spring Full Moon Festivals. Werner explained them to us. Since then I've seen them described in both Theosophic and Anthroposophic books. The information is also found on the internet. These three sacred Full Moon Festivals of Spring are important times when the spiritual energies focused on Earth are particularly strong. The first is the Festival of the Risen Sun (Son) or Easter. It's devoted to Christ and is at the Aries full moon of April.

The second of these three festivals is perhaps the most powerful. It is celebrated at the Taurus full moon of May, and is known as the Wesak Festival. It's the festival of Buddha. The third is celebrated at the Gemini full moon of June. This is the Festival of Goodwill and celebrates the spirit of humanity. The

Spiritual Hierarchy uses these festivals to strengthen, guide and awaken humanity toward spiritual *purpose.* These are very powerful times when the Hierarchy bestows special blessings on the Earth and humanity. Meditating at these times opens us to receive these concentrated blessings as individuals.

The first Full Moon Festival of April is the Easter Festival of the Risen Living Christ. He is the teacher of all men and the head of the Spiritual Hierarchy. He is also the expression of the Love of God.

The second festival of Wesak at the May full moon is very special because Buddha himself actually comes close to Earth at these times on the spiritual plane. There's a ceremony that takes place in a remote valley in the Himalayans near Mount Kailash. The Wesak is the festival of Buddha, the intermediary between the highest spiritual center of Shamballa and the Hierarchy. Buddha is the expression of the Wisdom of God, the Embodiment of Light and the divine purpose.

The third festival of Goodwill is the Festival of the spirit of humanity aspiring towards God. It is at these times human *will* seeks to unite with the will of God. At this festival the Christ has represented humanity for 2,000 years. Each year at that time He is said to preach the last sermon of the Buddha. It is for this reason an especially good day for invocation and a time for human and spiritual unity. I remember Werner saying that Christ and Buddha are very good friends and co-workers. They, along with other great spiritual beings and leaders, are all working toward the same goal of helping humanity to awaken.

In the early 1980s, I was living in Aspen, Colorado. At a library book sale I found an intriguing old set of leather-bound books called *Life and Teachings of the Masters of the Far East* by Baird Spalding. I later read that those books find their way to those who have known the Masters. If you have them, you have known the Masters in previous lives.

A few years after getting the books they were stolen. Decades later, in May of 2008, I happened to be talking to a friend Cheryl about the Masters. I said there were people who hiked the Himalayas to meet them in the 1800s, and I told her about Baird T. Spalding's books which I no longer had.

"If only I still had those books!" I said. "I'd like to read them again", and I sat there wishing I still had them.

A few days later I was driving south on a highway with my friend Susan. It had just stopped raining when suddenly there was the *MOST astounding* neon-bright rainbow on the left side of the road opposite our car as we drove south. It was the *most magnificent* rainbow we had ever seen! The band of it was *SO* vivid and *wide* that the orange side went all the way into violet. The green side extended into blue and then violet! It was incredible! Like an illustration in a children's book!" We thought for sure we'd see it on the news or in the paper the following day.

When we turned east was when the whole episode really got amazing. Now that magnificent rainbow was going *across* the highway. One end of it was on our right, and the other end was on our left! We seemed to drive right through it, when suddenly the sky lightened up and it was *GONE!* We had been so mesmerized with this other-worldly rainbow, it was only then this occurred to us. We realized that this magnificent sight had been beside our car for over an hour!

We were shocked to find nothing about it either on the news or the paper the next day. I couldn't help but wonder if anyone else had seen it. The next day, while walking my dog in front of the library, I saw they were having a book sale. I hadn't been to one in a while, not wanting to spend money. This particular day, however, I *knew* I *had* to go. I sensed there was something at the book sale *for me.* So I went back when the library opened and went directly to a table to discover a complete new five-piece set of *Life and Teachings of the Masters of the Far East!* I was amazed, and I walked home kind of lost in a reverie of the past few days. "Were they donated a few days ago, prompted by our conversation and my wishing for them?" I thought. "Or did I bring them up in the first place because I subconsciously picked up that they were there at the library next door?"

The thoughts of our unusual weekend kept running through my head. It seemed like that rainbow was somehow connected to the books. And then I realized it was the Wesak Festival weekend! Wesak is the most sacred time of the year to Theosophists, Anthroposophists, Hindus and Buddhists. It's one of the Spring Full Moon Festivals when the Masters come closest to Earth and humanity. It was such a strange and interesting series of events to have happened then.

24

Halfway To Heaven

It was May of 1964 and I was a petite 9-year-old. My best friend and I were on our way home from school one day when I found two pennies in my purse. Perfect for penny candy, and there happened to be a little neighborhood market across the street that sold it!

So we crossed the street, bought our candy and came back out to the curb. I didn't see or hear any cars coming and thinking there was no traffic, I ran to the other side of the street. What I remember is running toward a bush on the other side, when suddenly in the middle of the street the bush vanished. In an instant I wasn't there anymore. I was somewhere else. It seemed like I was just "pulled" from my body and blacked out.

The ladies in the beauty salon next door to the market saw it all from the salon's large window. They saw a child get struck by a car and the little body was thrown a hundred feet into the air, landing on its head.

The strange part was that my body landed in a totally limp state. And there *wasn't a scratch*! No cuts. No broken bones! Not even a scratch.

The doctors were baffled. From the distance I had been catapulted through the air, landing on my head, I should have broken every bone in my body and be dead. The *only* way it could have turned out the way it did, they said, would be *if* I was unconscious *before* impact. And that's exactly what happened.

I remember coming to consciousness as people were frantically shoving me into the back of an ambulance. It was all so surreal! I tried to sit up, but was pushed to lay back down.

"What in the *world* is *going on*?" I thought. I couldn't understand this abrupt change. In the midst of an ordinary afternoon, I was suddenly surrounded by a flurry of rushing people who seemed in a panic. When we arrived at the hospital and they wheeled me into the emergency room, I briefly came to consciousness again and tried one more time to sit up. For the second time I was pushed to lie down by another flurry of rushing people. That's when I went unconscious and I remained in what was called a "coma" for two weeks.

At first what I experienced in that unconscious state was a monotonous endless replay of the last few minutes before the impact. This scene played *OVER* and *OVER* again in minute detail, as if I were watching it all on a broken recording. I saw myself finding two pennies in my purse and crossing the street with my friend to get candy from the little store. I saw *exactly* what we chose, and even *which* shelves our candy came from. Molly chose a piece of bubble gum from the third shelf, and I chose a Black Jack from the second shelf. Then we'd get out to the curb and I'd run. I'd get halfway across the street, and then it would stop and "replay" *OVER* and *OVER* endlessly!

This eternal monotony could have lasted thirteen of the fourteen days I was unconscious. Then the scene abruptly changed. I suddenly found myself in a totally different setting. I was leaning against the trunk of a tree beside a lovely flowing brook. Along the other side of this little river were rolling green hills dotted with majestic Roman Cypress trees. They're the tall, thin fir trees that look like serene flames shaped like poplar trees. (It's interesting that in ancient spiritual paintings those trees are often used in scenes of the afterlife. It makes me wonder if someone had seen them on "the other side".)

To my right there was a quaint arched bridge over this brook. After a little while I walked down to the bridge and crossed it. It was such a pretty place. I went a short way up the nearest hill just to my left and sat leaning against the trunk of the closest Cypress tree.

I was enjoying the peaceful scenery when something unexpected happened. Someone stepped out from behind the closest tree to my left and began walking toward me. He had a very special quality that was almost magnetizing to me, and he seemed so familiar too. It felt like I had known him sometime in the distant past.

In the few moments it took for this man to reach me, I had made up my mind I wanted to go back with him. I don't know how I knew this, but it was clear to me this man had come from somewhere far out in the universe, and I had such a strong desire to go back with him. You'd think, as a young child, I'd want to return to my own family. But there was something SO special about this man. I really wanted to go with him! He seemed more important to me than my own mom or dad.

In those few moments while he was walking toward me, thoughts shot through my mind with instant images. I thought about where he was from, and instantly I *knew* that he was from a distant place far off in the universe, and I saw it in stages. First I saw the distant star. It was way out in the distance behind me ... off behind my right shoulder and slightly up. Then I zeroed in on a view of his home. It was a LOVELY white gleaming palace of a building. Then suddenly I was seeing his home from the inside, as if I were standing in the entryway. There were second floor balconies overlooking the front room, creating a peaceful courtyard effect.

This kind person sat down beside me in front of this tree. He knew exactly what I had been thinking. We talked, and all the

212

while he was trying to convince me to return to Earth. He said there was more for me to do there. I don't remember many details about the conversation, but I DO remember talking about my life and what I had been doing. He seemed pleased with my life. (I was the type of kid who loved to tell stories and make people happy.)

And then he said, "The *most important* thing of our *ENTIRE LIVES* is the happiness we share with others".

Years later I would think about that statement and realize what he meant was the *Love* we share with others. Happiness is a much easier concept for a child to grasp.

So there I was in this peaceful place talking with this incredible "person". He kept trying to convince me to return to Earth. He said there was more for me to do there, and that I would be with him "soon". At the end of our conversation he pointed with his right arm slightly up and to the right. A square patch of sky where he was pointing became black, and we could see the stars there. He was pointing to the brightest one, and I knew that was Earth.

Then I woke up in Intensive Care and amazed everyone. By then I had received the Last Rites three times, maybe because my father was a doctor and the priest wanted to be as helpful as he could. No one expected me to live. I'd think about the place I had "visited" many times over the years since then. If it was real distances, and not just a projection, then the bright star he pointed to would be Venus. Earth and Venus are roughly the same size, and they'd appear about the same from either place -- as the brightest "star" in the sky.

Stopping off after death

Years later Werner explained that our "stopping off" place after we excarnate or die, is Venus on another dimension or plane. We go over our life and what we had done in the life we just left with a spiritual guide on a different dimension of Venus.

Werner had something interesting to say about my near-death experience. He looked at me one day with those deep, intense eyes of his and said in his unforgettable British accent, "It wasn't an actual 'coma' that you were in. Rather, your body was 'on hold' while decisions were being made elsewhere."

The statement was both mysterious and understandable. And it was clear to me that he had *viewed* it all and spoke with insightful knowledge. That long monotonous replay I experienced certainly seems to fit an "on hold" pattern. However, it still leaves me wondering what decisions were being made while I was in the "on hold" position. Maybe he meant my decision whether or not to return to Earth. But I still wonder if other "decisions were being made *elsewhere*." He made another enigmatic statement. He said it was destiny for me to be "on the other side" on that date, but that It didn't have to be so bad and have such traumatic effects.

I've wished over the years I had asked him what had made it "so bad". Not that it would matter at this point, but I've been curious. With people like that, you have to ask the right questions

214

to get the answers you want though. "You didn't ask the right question, 'Grasshopper'!" I've thought to myself.

Werner found it interesting that my near-death experience happened in May. I always wondered why he found that so interesting. His only comment was it was *meant* to happen then, and he implied I was destined to be *on the other side* that day. It left me curious about why the timing would have been significant. Not long ago I did a search to find when the Wesak Full Moon of that year would have been. Sure enough! It happened to fall on that date. It still doesn't answer the question of exactly why I was destined to be "on the other side" on that day, but that's what happened.

Life holds many mysteries. Our real journey begins as we discover and investigate them. It is a quest that broadens our understanding and expands our awareness. I hope this book has helped solve some of these mysteries and that it has sparked a curiosity to explore other areas of sacred space.

Kristen Ann

Resources and Books

Tours to Egypt and other Sacred Places

<u>SpiritQuestTours.com:</u> Located in Egypt. Tour guides are Emil Shaker and Mohammed Nazmy.

<u>Power Places Tours:</u> Offices located in the U.S.

Learning Centers and Sources:

<u>Free Soul:</u> A center for learning and higher awareness. Started by Pete Sanders, in Sedona AZ.

<u>Share International</u>: Devoted to the Emergence of the Masters. www.share-international.org

<u>Sunbridge Institute:</u> Current name of the Waldorf Teacher Training Institute. www.Sunbridge.edu

<u>Transmission Meditation</u> details and info on joining a group: www.TramsmissionMeditation.org

<u>Flower of Life information:</u> www.world-mysteries.com/sar_sage1.htm

<u>Thrive Movie:</u> Highly recommended for an in-depth picture of life on planet Earth. www.ThriveMovement.com

Books:

<u>Atwater, F. Holmes</u>: *Captain of My Ship, Master of My Soul*

<u>Bailey, Alice</u>: Written for the serious spiritual student. She has written dozens of fascinating books, all containing information given from the Masters to help humanity. *Esoteric Psychology Vol. I* explains the rays. We each have different dominant rays, and understanding them helps us to know what we need to work on in this life. It's one among many of her intriguing books.

Bardon, Franz: *Frabato The Magician, Memories of Franz Bardon,* available from www.MerkurPublishing.com.

Besant, Annie: *The Ancient Wisdom, Esoteric Christianity, The Masters* and thirty-seven other books.

Blavatsky, Helena: *The Secret Doctrine, Isis Unveiled.*

Bourgault, Luc: *The American Indian Secrets of Crystal Healing*

Braden, Gregg: Gregg has written many books.

Cayce, Edgar: *Egypt, Parts I and II,* along with many other fascinating books including a compilation from his readings called *Gems and Stones.*

Cott, Jonathan: *The Search for Omm Sety.*

Creme, Benjamin: *Transmission Meditation, The Ageless Wisdom Teaching: An Introduction to Humanity's Spiritual Legacy.* Many others including three volumes of *Maitreya's Mission.*

Fry, Daniel: *The White Sands Incident.* See DanielFry.com

Haich, Elisabeth: *Initiation.*

Hall, Judy: *Crystal Bible, Crystal Bible 2.*

Kosmos Journal: Kosmos is a magazine that I *highly recommend.* www.KosmosJournal.org. Founded in 2001, Kosmos is the leading international Journal for planetary citizens committed to a new planetary culture.

MacDonald-Bayne, Murdo: *Beyond The Himalayas, The Yoga Of The Christ,* and many more. About meeting the Masters. www.murdomacdonald-bayne.com

McMoneagle, Joe: *The Ultimate Time Machine* and others.

McMullen, George: *Born Many Times, One White Crow, Red Snake, Running Bear: Grandson of Red Snake, Two Faces: Walking In Two Worlds.*

Morehouse, David: *Psychic Warrior* and others.

Raphael, Katrina: *Crystal Enlightenment Vol. I, Crystal Healing Vol. II, The Crystalline Transmission Vol. III,* and others.

Roerich, Helena: *The Agni Yoga Teachings.* AgniYoga.org.

Roerich, Nicholas: Husband of Helena. There's a Roerich Museum in NYC. Among his images are some of Maitreya. American-Buddha.com/nicholas.roerich.htm.

Schnabel, Jim: *Remote Viewers: The Secret History of America's Psychic Spies.*

Schwartz, Stephan: *The Secret Vaults of Time: Psychic Archaeology and the Quest for Man's Beginnings,* and *The Alexandria Project.*

Simmons, Robert: *The Book of Stones*

Sitchin, Zecharia: *Chariots of the Gods* and others.

Spalding, Baird T.: *Life And Teachings Of The Masters of the Far East.* A series of five books. A sixth was also added more recently.

Steiner, Rudolf: *Theosophy, Outline of Occult Science, How to Know Higher Worlds,* just to mention a few. He has written dozens of fascinating books. Written for the serious student of spiritual science. Not easy reading, but wonderful information.

Tart, Charles T.: *The Ultimate Time Machine,* co-authored with Joe McMoneagle. Other books also including *The End of Suffering,* written with J. J. Hurtak.

Tellinger, Michael: *Adam's Calendar, Slave Species of god, Temples of the African gods.*

Thompson Smith, Angela: *Diary of an Abduction, Remote Perceptions: Out-of-Body Experiences, Remote Viewing, and Other Normal Abilities.*

About the Author

Kristen has spent a lifetime studying spirituality and metaphysics. Her life has been filled with unusual experiences, encounters and constant synchronicities or "coincidences". These have added depth to her understanding of life at its core levels.

She had a near-death experience as a child which brought an awareness that there are many more levels of existence than the physical one we see. It also deepened Kristen's natural sense of curiosity to learn the deepest truths of existence. She began her lifelong quest as a child, reading any spiritual and metaphysical books she could find, starting in the mid 1960s. This included books by Edgar Cayce, Jean Dixon and Ruth Montgomery among others.

In the mid 1970s Kristen studied the research and findings of the profound clairvoyant Rudolf Steiner at the Waldorf Teacher Training Institute. Steiner created the spiritual science called Anthroposophy, which presents deepest truths of existence and spirituality.

Since the 1970s studies have continued in many different areas of life, spirituality, and the ultimate potentials, purpose and destiny of humanity.

Other areas of interest include painting, sculpture, playing a Celtic harp, piano, wooden alto recorder and native American flutes.